Ivan Spencer has put together a brilliant and creative introduction to the profoundly influential thought of Friedrich Nietzsche. Placing Nietzsche's sayings in the contemporary context of the Twittersphere, Spencer has not only made this nineteenth-century German philosopher's work accessible to modern readers, he has provided thoughtful, reflective, and significantly helpful interpretation as well. Spencer's work is commendable on many levels, but the truly important contribution of this book can be found in Spencer's insightful analysis of the worldview implications of Nietzsche's thought. I highly recommend this fine work.

DAVID S. DOCKERY, President, Trinity International University

Ivan Spencer's *Tweetable Nietzsche* is the liveliest and fastest-paced introduction to Friedrich Nietzsche's thought that one could wish for. Anyone who reads this book will be informed, instructed, and entertained.

BRUCE RILEY ASHFORD, Provost and Professor of Theology and Culture, Southeastern Baptist Theological Seminary

Ivan Spencer's *Tweetable Nietzsche* is absolutely fantastic! Nietzsche has been, and continues to be, one of the most important thinkers in the history of Western thought. Spencer does a masterful job of representing the major features of his thought and capturing his aphoristic style. For any student of philosophy or the history of ideas, this is an absolute must-read. I am delighted to see this great contribution to Nietzschean literature!

JAMES K. DEW JR., Associate and Philosophy, Southeastern Ba

I once wrote a paper titled "Why Nietzsche Was Right" in his criticisms of the church and so forth. Ultimately, I said he was "Wrong." This book by Ivan Spencer is also "Right" and certainly not wrong. By "Right" I mean really, really good. By "Wrong" I mean Nietzsche had a fallacious worldview. We need more books like this one, with its worldview orientation, specifically toward Nietzsche. And thank God for @TwilghtOfIdols and several other hashtags. If you read this work, you too can tweet Nietzsche in under 140 characters (including spaces) and perhaps develop a biblical worldview—one unlike Nietzsche's own. After all, he got things Wrong!

DAVID NAUGLE, THD, PHD, Chair and Professor of Philosophy, Distinguished University Professor, Dallas Baptist University; and author, *Worldview: The History of a Concept*

Tweetable
Nietzsche

Tweetable Nietzsche

HIS
ESSENTIAL
IDEAS
REVEALED
and
EXPLAINED

C. Ivan Spencer

ZONDERVAN®

ZONDERVAN

Tweetable Nietzsche
Copyright © 2016 by C. Ivan Spencer

This title is also available as a Zondervan ebook.

Requests for information should be addressed to:
Zondervan, *3900 Sparks Dr. SE, Grand Rapids, Michigan 49546*

Library of Congress Cataloging-in-Publication Data

Names: Spencer, C. Ivan (Charles Ivan), 1962-
Title: Tweetable Nietzsche : his essential ideas revealed and explained / C. Ivan Spencer.
Description: Grand Rapids, MI : Zondervan, 2016.
Identifiers: LCCN 2016023078 | ISBN 9780310000921 (softcover)
Subjects: LCSH: Nietzsche, Friedrich Wilhelm, 1844-1900.
Classification: LCC B3317 .S61955 2016 | DDC 193—dc23 LC record available at https://
    lccn.loc.gov/2016023078

Cover design: Tim Green / FaceOut Studio
Cover and interior photo: Gustav-Adolf Schultze / Wikimedia Commons
Interior design: Kait Lamphere
Editing: Katya Covrett, Audrey Enters, Bob Hudson

Printed in the United States of America

16 17 18 19 20 21 22 23 24 25 /DHV/ 15 14 13 12 11 10 9 8 7 6 5 4 3 2 1

Tammy, best friend in life,
godsend, and dear wife

Contents

Introduction

Imagine that the iconic and protean philosopher Friedrich Nietzsche returns from beyond to tweet his views on life, humanity, ethics, politics, religion, and a host of other issues. *Tweetable Nietzsche* distills the key elements from Nietzsche's discernable worldview into tiny quotes in the Twitter format as if he were alive today. Through his short and biting statements, we will quickly grasp the big picture of his worldview. After surveying tweets of his major themes, we'll dive into some deeper evaluations and implications.

Why Nietzsche?

On a Richter scale of thinkers, the Nietzschean earthquake ranks well above 9.0 with many serious aftershocks. Overestimation of his influence rarely occurs due to an ongoing domino effect he initiated not only in the arts and humanities but also in ethics, politics, and philosophy. Spawning diverse movements and followers, his brilliant flashes of intuition, wit, and pithy insights scan the human situation like an MRI of the brain, earning both praise and scorn from countless observers. Though prophetic in his cultural foresight, he perplexes most people with his counterintuitive contrarian style. Nietzsche inspires, mystifies, enthuses, agitates, or riles everyone who encounters him. You may agree or disagree with Nietzsche, but an understanding of his ideas allows deeper insight into our times because he pioneered many cultural developments of the past century.

The Twitter format fits Nietzsche like a glove because of his poignant and aphoristic style. If he were alive today, he would probably tweet his razor-sharp intuitions about the human situation. Viewing Nietzsche through a social-networking filter helps us understand his significance in our fast-paced world.

What is Twitter? Twitter connects people in a popular online social-networking environment that moves nimbly and quickly. When people "tweet," they broadcast a digital message of 140 characters or less from their phone, computer, or tablet. Twitter empowers a handful or a hundred million people to tune in to another person's tweets and "follow" their comments. Messages instantly envelop the globe. While Nietzsche is not actually here to tweet, we will follow him. If any #hashtags appear after the tweets, I have added those. Hashtags function as keywords on Twitter.

The idea for *Tweetable Nietzsche* emerged in 2013 out of my conversations with my daughters, colleagues, and my History of Ideas students. The need for an accessible introduction to Nietzsche for the social-networking savvy merged with a worldview study that fits his method.

Nietzsche's enigmatic life puzzles interpreters. He lived a lonely and painful life of both physical and emotional suffering. His last twelve years, ending in 1900, windswept his intellectual powers into a dark abyss of insanity.[1] Despite this tragic finale, he grew to an astonishing and cult-like fame, of which he remained oblivious. After his death, his legend enlarged to near-mythic proportions. Nietzsche's apotheosis into an archetype in Western culture epitomizes the eccentric, original, authentic, and tragic philosopher. What specific ideas does he epitomize?

Varied interpretations abound, compete, and multiply. Plainly an atheist, he often appears as a nihilist, an anarchist, a fascist, an elitist, an existentialist, a skeptic, a cynic, or a romantic. Many schools of thought claim Nietzsche is on their team. What does his overman, or superman (*Übermensch*), doctrine beckon us to embrace with his message of the eternal return? Some see the overman as a call to overcome struggles, to self-improvement, and to humanistic expression. Others see it as something darker, a call for a superior leader to overpower and dominate others. Did these ideas give rise to Nazism and the idea of a super-race, or did Nazis hijack his provocative ideas for their horrid agenda? Was he a cause for World Wars I and II? What does *will to power* mean? Since his death, his ideas enthrall and inspire audiences on a global scale with a style evoking a mystical and prophetic atheism. He unveils new and dangerous ideas such as the will to power, the overman, the eternal recurrence, the transvaluation of values, egoism, individualism, perspectivism, and amoralism. We will explore these questions and other topics as Nietzsche tweets his view of the world.

Nietzsche's work triggers myriad social, academic, political, and theological movements. Because no official version of Nietzsche ever emerged, his work supplies a prime matter to many visions. Steven Aschheim remarks, "Its elasticity and selective interpretive possibilities constituted its staying power and facilitated its infusion into so many areas of cultural and political life."[2] Nietzsche's writings often function as a Rorschach test in which people see what they intend to see or a vanity mirror from which one's face gazes back.

No single volume truly captures the giant scope of Nietzsche's works and interpretation. I will glean from the insights of some of the best scholars, but I will not attempt to reflect any particular interpretation of Nietzsche or school of thought. As an interpretive work, this book interacts primarily with Nietzsche, but I am not immune to errors of oversight, selection, and simplification. Any interpretation risks blind spots, but I endeavor to avoid them. At any rate, Nietzsche's ambiguity, obscurity, paradoxes, and chimerical pathos create pitfalls because he deliberately avoids creation of a system.

Nietzsche refuses to create a grand structure of ideas, and he dislikes the great philosophical system builders. His thought evolves and morphs over his life, but a pattern emerges. Employing aphorisms, his quirky and irreverent tone ensures that many generations will read him. Postmodernity echoes many of his sentiments and looks to him as a forerunner of its undermining of any privileged viewpoints. Never one to be rigorously consistent, and at times flouting logic, Nietzsche created counterintuitive observations and paradoxes. Some of his insights, such as the master-slave relationship, precede and anticipate psychoanalytic psychology. In his psychoanalysis of society, power, and traditional morality, he pinpoints many paradoxes of the human condition and pioneers the hermeneutics of suspicion.

The practicality of Nietzsche's ideas will prove insightful, though it can often only be applied subjectively. How do his insights relate to life? What implications arise if anyone should attempt to employ them? We'll explore a key issue for any philosophy: Can it be practiced? With all of his rants and riffs on innumerable topics, Nietzsche wants his principles to be followed in life. Ideas do have practical consequences.

While it will be impossible to fully interact with his complete philosophy from these espresso-strength tweets, they extract much of his essence. The problem of selecting the material to tweet looms, and probably few will agree with all of my selections. I attempt to include selections that best express his ideas while balancing them with a sense of tweetability. This survey cannot replace the reading of his works to fully grasp his worldview.[3] Before we probe Nietzsche's worldview, we need to explore what a worldview entails.

Worldviews and the Examined Life

What are worldviews and why do they matter? A worldview encapsulates a person's central assumptions and attitudes about the world and that person's commitments to them.[4] Our language, culture, upbringing, and perhaps even our genetics influence this system. If people were computers, the worldview would encode their operating systems. These deep assumptions, attitudes, and commitments guide our views of many other issues. For example, our everyday political views often flow from our deep assumptions about human nature. In turn, our views of human nature grow out of our assumption about the true nature of the universe.[5]

We construct and inform innumerable individual beliefs from a cluster of core assumptions. This whole process functions as our worldview. Someone might change an opinion or casual belief, but rarely do they change their core. Working toward a definition of worldviews, James Sire explains,

> A worldview is a commitment, a fundamental orientation of the heart, that can be expressed as a story or in a set of presuppositions (assumptions which may be true, partially true or entirely false) which we hold (consciously or subconsciously, consistently or inconsistently) about the basic constitution of reality, and that provides the foundation on which we live and move and have our being.[6]

Our buried cluster of assumptions provides the deepest motives or reasons for why we believe anything. You simply can't go any deeper. If you can, then what you uncover are the real assumptions driving things above. Not all our beliefs root into this basic level. I firmly believe that chocolate tastes best, but it isn't in my core and few things rely on that belief. However, if I unwittingly embrace the assumption that humans are only material beings with no soul, this will inform my judgments on ethical issues, social mores, politics, and much more. These principal assumptions function like genetic codes for thought, beliefs, and life commitments. They shape and instruct the details of our world vision even if we are unaware. Nietzsche scores superlative marks for intellectual honesty, depth, and accepting consequences. By analyzing Nietzsche's worldview we uncover why he thinks the way he does, identifying unseen and powerful drivers of his eminently influential world vision.

Such analysis imposes limits. It can't reveal every factor for someone's beliefs, yet it can reveal our inconsistencies and offer a multifaceted view that is rich and varied. Facing his death, Socrates unforgettably proclaimed, "The unexamined life is not worth living."[7] Can we live an examined life? Nietzsche did. To start, we must ask ourselves why we believe what we hold to be true. As we weave our web of beliefs, what do we anchor it to? If we keep asking why, digging deeper, we may find out. We will find some of Nietzsche's anchors. Uncovering our own worldview is not for the fainthearted because doing so can reveal major faults. Too often we live busy and unexamined lives, rarely knowing what drives our views of everything.

Nietzsche joins a few historical philosophers, prophets, poets, religious leaders, and politicians who have projected their worldview onto the minds and hearts of followers. Worldviews are not merely personal affairs but are socially transferred. Consider how Mohammed projected a worldview onto the minds and hearts of countless people. Most people subscribe to one of a few basic off-the-shelf worldview options that they customize to fit their needs. Nietzsche wanders through four worldviews in his lifetime. He began in life with a Christian (Lutheran) worldview but rejected it for naturalism as a young adult. Following naturalism led him inexorably to nihilism by carrying naturalism to a rigorous conclusion.[8] Nihilism bears down hard on the whole person and is hard to sustain. To crawl out of the despair of nihilism, Nietzsche originated some existentialist escape techniques. These last two worldviews, nihilism and existentialism, emerge from the womb of naturalism as fraternal twins. The three form a family. Nietzsche inspires a cultural shift toward this family. Thus naturalists, nihilists, and existentialists find inspiration and support in him. At times he appears to be one or another or all three. Naturalism entails an understanding of the world that says only matter and energy exist in a universe governed by natural laws. Sometimes the synonymous terms *materialism*, *atheism*, or *physicalism* will substitute for naturalism, depending on the context.

As I reveal Nietzsche's worldview I hope you will gain a deeper understanding into your own. We start with his understanding of what is most real, including the basic nature of the cosmos. Another important part of every worldview deals with knowledge, what it includes, and how we get it. Next we will encounter Nietzsche's earthshaking amoral vision of transvaluation. He said so much about morality that many think of him first as a moral philosopher. Morality leads to his understanding of human nature. We'll survey humanity separately because Nietzsche envisioned a new kind of human race with profound sociopolitical implications.

After human nature we explore Nietzsche's remarkable view of the will, where he develops groundbreaking perspectives with his famous doctrine of the will to power. We then investigate his view of death. Death opens the door to his peculiar view of the eternal return, another seminal doctrine. The eternal return in Nietzsche invites us to view our entire life story as an endlessly recurring replay, identical in each cycle. We will then survey some of Nietzsche's interesting glimpses on life and practical matters. In the last chapter, I offer some deeper reflections on his worldview. Using a threefold principle of unity will afford an understanding of Nietzsche that employs values he implicitly embraced. Finally, readers can begin to recognize his heavy influence on thinking in our times and assess his ideas when they reemerge.

Friedrich Nietzsche @TwilightOfIdols
This world is the will to power—and nothing besides! And you yourselves are also this will to power—and nothing besides![9]

↰   ⇄   ♥   •••

CHAPTER 1

Welcome to the Machine

The World As It Really Is

Friedrich Nietzsche @TwilightOfIdols
This world: a monster of energy, without beginning, without
end; a firm, iron magnitude of force that does not grow
bigger or smaller.[1]

W hat is the true nature of the universe? What is actually real? Nietzsche's answer consistently and emphatically denies any idea of a nonphysical, metaphysical, or transcendent world. Metaphysics studies these questions and ponders the question of a world beyond the physical one. Nietzsche's position leaves only the physical material world. To exist is to be physical. Soul, spirit, God, Supreme Being, and transcendence find no place in Nietzsche's materialism. Deeply impressed with F. A. Lange's influential work on materialism, he persistently attacks theistic worldviews that claim God created matter from nothing (*ex nihilo*) and caused everything physical to begin to exist.[2] Thus, Nietzsche overlooks many questions of final reality, yet he assumes materialism as the basic nature of all things while undermining the supernatural.

An old maxim among philosophers, "Either mind made matter, or matter made minds," expresses two fundamental metaphysical families:

idealism and materialism. A monist sees the whole world as one simple thing, meaning literally one-ism (mono). Both idealism and materialism embrace opposing monistic views, but a third view blends both mind and matter into a coeternally existing dualism. Either a Supreme Mind of some kind created the material world and our minds, or matter alone creates minds (for example, through the mechanism of the Big Bang and evolution). Nietzsche consistently and passionately believes matter made minds.

Few people muse about these grand questions of metaphysics, but we assume something about them. Worldview assumptions lie so deeply embedded that few people consciously think about them. It can be quite hard to uncover your assumptions and realize they influence your understanding. Why? They operate like the retina of your eye, allowing you to see all without seeing the retina. Metaphysics includes a range of deep questions about existence, being, and the nature of all things. A profound belief about what is really real lies embedded in us, where it quietly spins as the hub of our worldview. The word *metaphysics* combines two words: *after* + *physics*. The great philosopher Aristotle wrote a book about physics. He then wrote another book discussing the concepts of being, existence, essence, and first principles. His best-known first principle is the Unmoved Mover, the idea that all events in the cosmos must begin with or be caused by a Mover that initiates all motions. Lacking a name, Aristotle's book became known as *Metaphysics*, literally after the book *Physics*, being the second in a series. Eventually the term *metaphysics* came to mean the kinds of topics found in Aristotle's book. Now the name designates a study of the nonphysical world, first principles, and the world of pure ideas, concepts, essence, and universals. Sounds fun!

In the tweets that follow, we will see multifrontal assaults from Nietzsche on metaphysical concepts. Like many other philosophers since that age, he abandons metaphysics and denies any reality outside, above, or beyond the natural world.

Now we begin with what is perhaps his most famous tweet.

Friedrich Nietzsche @TwilightOfIdols

God is dead. God remains dead. And we have killed him.[3]

#Godisdead #WekilledGod

One of the most famous *TIME* magazine covers, April 8, 1966, in bold red letters asks, "Is God Dead?" The lead article remarks, "No longer is the question the taunting jest of skeptics for whom unbelief is the test of wisdom and for whom Nietzsche is the prophet who gave the right answer a century ago."[4] While the Death of God theology of the '60s waned quickly, the specter of God's demise will haunt the ensuing decades.

In his famous and autobiographical passage, "The Madman," Nietzsche's mouthpiece prophetically shouts an incendiary sermon. The madman descends from a mountain abode to a marketplace proclaiming his message about God's death and its unrealized consequences. The shocked people hearing the message do not realize the full consequences of living in their self-chosen secular society. They write stolen checks to each other that draw on closed bankrupt accounts. They refuse to see that the Christian values and morals they still cling to have no basis. If the madman is right, the pitiful values rooted in God must be purged, but people sheepishly cling to them because they are too weak to create their own individualistic values.

In Nietzsche's day naturalism surged to a new height boosted by Darwin's theories. To Nietzsche, belief in God, the central hub of Western civilization's ideas and culture, thwarts progress. R. J. Hollingdale says, "Nietzsche accepted the fundamental implication of Darwin's hypothesis, namely that mankind had evolved in a purely naturalistic way through chance and accident."[5] The Jewish and Christian idea of God wilts away and loses viability for post-Darwin European civilization. The hub is gone, even though the wheel may briefly spin on. People don't realize the full implications of their killing of God, nor have they followed the consequences out to their appropriate conclusion.

The madman character parallels the prophet Zarathustra in Nietzsche's great lyrical work, *Thus Spoke Zarathustra*. He names the prophet after Zoroaster, the historical founder of the Zoroastrian religion. Zarathustra at one time believed in a dualistic view of the universe where good and evil struggled. He abandoned that dualistic disaster for a new vision. As Nietzsche's mouthpieces, both the madman and Zarathustra descend from their mountain isolation to declare the consequences of the death of God and the ensuing naturalistic vision of the world with its revamped and revised value system.

The gradual sunset of God in our culture lingers on today, but for many the sun sank into darkness long ago. Since Nietzsche's lifetime, fewer and fewer people see God as sufficient for explaining any aspect of the world. A growing sociological group called "nones," a term for people who have mostly no or very low interest in any religion, expands and agrees.[6] Nietzsche would be elated with the increasing acceptance of materialist thinking today.

In naturalism the inescapable laws of nature cause everything in the universe and sufficiently explain all of reality. For things that science cannot yet explain, naturalists do not invoke God. To do so is to fall into a "God of the gaps" fallacy because science will soon understand the unexplainable. Naturalists persist in scientific investigation believing that every mysterious phenomenon will reveal its natural causes.

Nietzsche's death of God tweet echoes through our culture.[7] God is now less relevant to life than Santa—he explains nothing! To say God is dead, however, or to ask whether there has ever been a God, carries far weightier consequences than the loss of a holiday figure. Nietzsche fully and intentionally grasped the consequences. Even if we disagree, his intellectual honesty in accepting the implications merits attention. If we killed God and removed him from our culture, then all the corresponding values that derive from God die too: heaven and hell, objective good and evil, absolute right and wrong, justice and injustice, and free will and responsibility, just to name a few. This is what the people don't get about the madman's marketplace prophecy. They killed God, but they want to keep the core values dependent on God, values around which their social world spins.

As we will see, the death of God in Nietzsche's thought reaches into most other areas of his philosophy. Erich Heller remarks, "This is the very core of Nietzsche's spiritual existence, and what follows is despair *and* hope in a new greatness of man."[8] We'll soon see unrelenting chain reactions that start with God's death.

Friedrich Nietzsche @TwilightOfIdols

When gods die, they always die several kinds of death . . . This way or that, this way and that—he is gone![9]

The gods of many past civilizations have died, and those civilizations have died too. Few gods still occupy the center of a culture, but there are some, such as Islamic societies. Nietzsche did not believe that God once lived, aged, and then died. Rather, God never existed and is a quaint cultural notion that withers away like belief in Zeus. In the past, the idea of Zeus captivated Greek culture and infused it with meaning. The wheel of society spun around the hub of Zeus. As that idea faded and died with the rise of Greek philosophy, Greek culture shifted.

How can gods die? They can be physically destroyed when their images are destroyed. Conquerors regularly demolished idols. Gods can die when people lose faith in them or when they stop worshiping the gods. When one civilization falls in defeat to another stronger civilization, the religion of the vanquished may well die. Any culture rooted in a god dies when the idea of that god dies.

Naturalists might agree that religion once played a role in social evolution, helping us advance into cooperative societies of a unified purpose. Nietzsche says religion must now go because its deadweight drags humanity down. Atheists today mostly agree, and heartily. As we will see below, Nietzsche reasons that all belief in gods, the supernatural, the metaphysical, and religions will die because a superior cultural movement renders it useless and even harmful. He thinks religious belief, especially Jewish and Christian, lingers as an illusion unworthy of enlightened minds who should see that religion was just a phase of development from beast to human. He says much less about Islam, but there's no reason to think he would see it differently. Regardless, now humans must continue to evolve. Nietzsche poses his ideas as a catalyst for the next major stage in human evolution.

Friedrich Nietzsche @TwilightOfIdols

The belief in the Christian God has ceased to be believable . . . is even now beginning to cast its first shadows over Europe.[10]

A recent Pew Foundation study confirms the decline Nietzsche here prophesies; Christianity in Europe today decreases every year.[11] The global center of Christianity drifts farther away from Europe and North America each year. For Europe and North America's increasingly secular society, many cease to find God believable. A WIN-Gallup international poll on religion shows a 9% global drop in religious belief and a 3% rise in atheism between 2005 and 2011, merely six years.[12] A 2015 Pew Research poll confirms this growing trend.[13] Most of this decline occurs where Nietzsche's prescient tweet said it would. What did he grasp that others didn't?

In *The Gay Science*, Nietzsche quips that if everyone realizes and accepts that there is no God or afterlife, and no moral rules, then humanity can finally spread its wings and fly. When the deadweight of religion falls off, humanity will run faster. Most atheists through the ages claim that we can finally live life-affirming goals instead of life-robbing traditional values that exact high costs with no benefit. In enthusiasm, he writes, "We philosophers and 'free spirits' feel as if a new dawn were shining on us when we receive the tidings that 'the old god is dead'; our heart overflows with gratitude, amazement, anticipation, expectation."[14]

We will launch our ships on open seas and live with daring, danger, and courage. Nietzsche's giddiness over the prospect that there is no God dominating humanity echoes ancient ideas.

Ancient materialists, such as the Epicureans, foreshadowed Nietzsche's excitement over the prospect of living and dying without God, without morals or the threat of eternal punishment. In his incredible book *The Nature of Things*, written about 50 BCE, Lucretius explained Epicurean atomism, an ancient form of materialism. He argued that people could live blissfully knowing that when they die, there is no judgment in the afterlife, no punishment to fear. He exhorts, "Know that there's nothing for us to fear in death, that a man who doesn't exist can't be unhappy, that for him it's just as if he'd never been born."[15] Lucretius, like Nietzsche two millennia later, urges us to live in the moment—like there is no tomorrow. With no gods to serve, people experience liberation in life and death. It saves them psychological turmoil from fear, money, and time spent in devotion to the gods. Historical materialists from antiquity to Nietzsche bear remarkable similarities.

Popular atheists today often distance themselves from the historical materialists and from Nietzsche, even though he was atheism's first rock star. They share kindred spirits, but their agenda and methods differ. Even though Nietzsche's knowledge about the natural world pales in comparison to that of current naturalists, he injected a plausible disbelief into many and advanced a secular age.

The secular age welcomes the elongating shadows of the setting sun of God. Twilight sets quickly. People increasingly abandon their search for a transcendent meaning and settle in to the monotone drone of life in the machine age. Our personal value and identity often depend largely on our decreasing ability to perform services that society values.

In our quest for significance, Nietzsche believes that once people's minds are liberated, they can genuinely live, unburdened by religious claptrap. Yet an existence void of transcendent meaning leaves many feeling empty. Nietzsche expects them to invent their own meaning. Out of the bleak desert lands of the God-free cosmos, he urges individuals to will an oasis of meaning. This spirit of triumphal overcoming through the will catapulted Nietzsche to the status of a cultural prophet and poet.

Friedrich Nietzsche @TwilightOfIdols
Once to sin against God was the greatest sin; but God died, and these sinners died with him.[16]

↩   ↻   ♥   •••

What could *sin* possibly mean in an atheistic worldview? If God dies, then sin dies too. In theistic worldviews, *sin* means "to fall short, to miss the mark, to be deficient." In all theisms, sin entails any moral deficiency. Since God defines moral standards, *to sin* means "to fall short of God's expectations." In Nietzsche's atheistic view, there can be no sin per se, because no God exists to define the moral standards for sin. You can't sin any more than you can stop being a dolphin. The category does not apply.

We rarely hear of sin in nonreligious contexts, but when we do, the word becomes a metaphor for socially flawed moral activity. Perhaps sin connotes breaking a law, a crime, misbehavior, a *faux pas,* or a breach of social contract. However, the word *sin* carries an outmoded, passé connotation that one has somehow offended the Creator of the universe by breaking his moral laws. As God dies, with him, the concept of sinners die.

Friedrich Nietzsche @TwilightOfIdols
Christianity is Platonism "for the people."[17]

↩   ↻   ♥   •••

For Nietzsche, Christianity hatched the egg Plato laid—and raised a barnyard of chickens. Plato says transcendent mental ideas (the Forms) exist and that material objects simply reflect them. As ephemeral projections, material things such as trees, houses, animals, and humans merely shadow Plato's eternal ideas. If you've ever seen the movie *The Matrix,* you get the idea. The physical world is Plato's Matrix, at least in my viewing. Nietzsche's materialism strictly opposes Plato's idealism. In a celebrated passage in the *Republic*, Plato illustrates his unearthly philosophy through a vivid story of a man imprisoned in a cave.[18]

A prisoner bound by chains in a deep cave views only a wall in front of where he is chained with others. On this wall flitter shadows projected by objects free people held in front of a fire far behind the prisoner that he can't see. All that the man has ever seen or known comes from these shadows. Over the course of his life, the prisoner believes that the shadows are all that exist.

One day the prisoner's chains slip off. He crawls out from the prison and beholds the free people, the objects they carry, and the fire making the shadows. Shocked by this revelation, he then discovers a pathway out of the cave into the unknown but brilliant upper world. He staggers up into the blinding light. At the surface, a stunning reality strikes him. The sky, clouds, land, and trees astound him. He finally beholds the true source of all light, all truth, all beauty, and all knowledge: the Sun. This revelation transforms him. He knows he must liberate others. Elatedly he descends back into the shadows. Intent on delivering his fellow prisoners from the lies they believe, from the shadows, he proclaims the good news. Hearing his bizarre story, they laugh, mock, and vilify him. Upon realizing his story would upend everything they always thought to be true, the other prisoners murder him. Many interpreters see the prisoner as Socrates, a philosopher who gave up his life in a martyr-like fashion, trying to enlighten others.

Plato's story etches an idealistic worldview on the soul of Western civilization where truth, meaning, and reality transcend the cave of this material world. Alfred North Whitehead famously stated, "The safest general characterization of the European philosophical tradition is that it consists of a series of footnotes to Plato."[19] The material world people think of as reality merely consists of shadows, faint wisps, and reflections of a real world above, beyond, and outside the cave of matter. For Plato and most forms of Christianity, the real world is spiritual, mental, nonmaterial, and composed of pure ideas. Nietzsche strives to change the European footnotes to Plato. Always affirming the physical, the natural, and the body with its pleasures, Nietzsche vigorously accuses Christianity of teaching the same thing as Plato. Like Plato, some forms of Christianity minimize the role and importance of this material world in favor of another world. Some Christians who long for heaven look upon this physical world and the body with scorn and disrespect. For Nietzsche, this otherworldly vision sucks the life out of us and brings nihilism, a kind of living death.

Much of Nietzsche's writing opposes Christianity, not just his stirring work *The Antichrist*, which is a full-frontal assault. In equating Christianity with Greek Platonism, he accuses the pair of two things. First, as an antiquated vision of the world thriving in dark times, mystical Platonism offered no benefits to humanity; it thwarted authentic progress by shifting everyone's focus to another world. The winding road to the dead end of platonic idealism ended the essentialist mind-set. Post-Darwin materialism allows nothing to have an essence because that's metaphysical. The nineteenth century drank the Kool-Aid of modernity's progress and belittled belief in a transcendent world.

Second, classic Christianity shares guilt by association because it parallels Platonism. In Nietzsche's mind, Christianity is Plato wearing Christian garb. If Christianity teaches the same otherworldly and Earth-hating nonsense as Platonism, then Christianity perpetuates humanity's struggle. For Nietzsche, the lies about fictional worlds with a proverbial "pie in the sky, by and by" place deadweights around humanity's neck. Rejecting both, Nietzsche identifies with that prisoner from Plato's cave, but he delivers a radical message: stay chained up in the cave—there's nothing outside to see—deal with it.

CHAPTER 2

What Do You Really Know?

Lies, Damned Lies

Nietzsche's perspective on knowledge and truth may surprise us, but our era mirrors many of his inclinations. Epistemology explores how we obtain knowledge. What is knowledge? Why and how can we know reliably? These questions still puzzle humanity after thousands of years, and many have abandoned the quest for a grand theory of knowledge. Philosophers have all answered these questions quite differently, and epistemological debate raged through long periods of Western civilization's history. The modern age, starting around 1640 with the philosophy of Descartes, intensified epistemological investigations. Two basic positions, evolved from ancient times, rivaled each other: empiricism and rationalism. We will look at both in their basic forms.

Empiricism claims that knowledge begins in the five senses. Seeing is believing. Empirical knowledge, obtained by observing and experiencing the physical world, now dominates our age in the increasingly sophisticated methods of modern science. Each scientific method appeals to some type of empirical knowledge. Each renders probable knowledge and enables predictions of outcomes, though not certainty. When people say that science rules, they usually mean that empirical methods of gaining probable knowledge surpass any other way. Philosophers refer to empirical knowledge as *aposteriori* because it comes after experience of the world.

Rationalism holds that knowledge emerges from careful reasoning through rational operations in the mind. Reason unlocks or recovers buried knowledge. This innate knowledge does not arrive through the senses. Rationalists distrust the easily confused senses that, at best, give a vague inkling of reality. Rational knowledge attains certainty. Two plus two equals four. No sensory observation helps or is required. Such clear and certain knowledge emerges from mental processes independent of the senses. Philosophers refer to such knowledge as *apriori* because it arises prior to experiences of the world.

Empiricism and rationalism evolved into many variations and combinations. Serious attempts to unify them, such as Immanuel Kant's, retain the two positions' insights into our quest for knowledge. To understand Nietzsche, we must grasp Kant's grand fusion of these two epistemologies in the decades preceding Nietzsche.

Kant blends both approaches, claiming our minds contain rational categories (*apriori*) that filter all observations (*aposteriori*). We see an apple fall and we know there must be a cause, even if we don't observe that cause. A dog could see the apple fall but never know its cause. Canines possess senses vastly superior to ours, but our complex minds innately contain and impose a rational understanding on experiences. *All experiences conform to the human mind, not vice versa.* This summarizes Kant's Copernican revolution. We process every sensation through hardwired filters of human nature, such as the "cause" filter. Thus we automatically presuppose any event has a cause. Our cause filter preconditions our understanding such that we impose it on all sensory events. Kant identified fourteen of these filters. When we speak of intuitions, we often refer to these automated preconceptions that we may only be vaguely aware of.

Humanity's incessant desire to discover causes lies at the core of the scientific quest and our ability to control nature for our purposes. The empirical part of Kant's blended system comes from simple observations. Seeing the apple fall provides the sensory part; our mind processing that data through the grid of filters supplies the rational part. Without the sensory part, the rational part lies empty, but without the rational part, the sensory part has no structure. Why did Kant explain things this way? A dangerous specter of skepticism had reemerged, thanks to David Hume, who taught a radical form of empiricism. Hume's skepticism would kill all knowledge. Nihilism loomed.

Hume taught that we could never know the cause of anything since we can only roughly predict and give probabilities. For Hume, knowledge falls from certainty to mere possibilities, as unreliable as predicting the weather. He undermined modern science's ability to discover and manipulate causes in the natural world. Dangerous indeed. Progress would halt. Kant said Hume "first interrupted my dogmatic slumbers."[1] Kant arose to solve the epistemological quandary upsetting modernity.

Nietzsche understands the tensions between rationalism and empiricism and Kant's epic attempt to synthesize them. He also grasps that Kant's epistemology, for all its attempts to divert Hume's skepticism, also risks succumbing to it. For in Kant's view, even if we rationally organize them, we only know our private experiences, never the true nature of things. We can never know how red appears to another person. We can't experience redness or rose in itself, only our private sensation of a particular rose.

Nietzsche acknowledges Kant's epistemology and accepts it through the unique lens of Arthur Schopenhauer, history's arch-pessimist. The rationalists, empiricists, and Kant engineered philosophical wheels with epistemology as the hub. Following Schopenhauer's cue, Nietzsche redesigns those wheels with the will as the hub, demoting knowledge to the rim. Something more primal and basic precedes and dominates our pursuit of knowledge: the will. The redesigned wheel powers existentialism. Will drives knowledge. We alone press the shape of our will into the passive wax of nature. Who cares if water is wet? I can will to dry it up or freeze it. Will precedes, drives, and rules over knowledge, truth, values, and even science. Will constructs all, so systems of truth and knowledge should never rule over the individual will. This radical recalibration of the wheel's hub may not be clear to you yet, but it revolutionizes the world. Many of philosophy's footnotes now point to Nietzsche, not Plato.

Friedrich Nietzsche @TwilightOfIdols

What, then is truth? . . . Truths are illusions about which one has forgotten that this is what they are.[2]

Nietzsche invites us to imagine the entire human situation and all of human history as a brief gasp in the cosmos. On a lonely speck of a planet circling a star among innumerable solar systems, some smart animals invented something they called knowledge. This tiny yet incredible cosmic moment begins and then ends as the star burns out. The animals die. The end.

In case you missed it, we are the animals.

For Nietzsche, our intellect fabricates knowledge to survive. Knowledge merely serves our self-centered survival interests. What do humans really know about themselves? What we call knowledge is really a mixing pot of lies, deceptions, and fantasies for self-preservation. We can't see ourselves as we really are, as beasts intent on savagery. Why does the human animal seek knowledge and what is it good for? Our quest for knowledge is a ruse to gain advantage over others. However, we want to cohabit with others, so we create social contracts for peace.

At this moment of social organization, we contract to use words as "truth." Human societies socially construct truth (and deception) for survival benefits, but they have no interest in pure knowledge. The words we employ do not embody knowledge but are only conventions, mere nerve stimulation in sounds. Words have no meaning and convey no truth. Truth is a social convention itself, like the sounds of the words of so many languages. The "thing in itself," or the brute fact of reality, can't be known or embodied in words.

Nietzsche follows nominalism to extremes. Nominalism says no universals exist; only particular things exist that we give a name. What are words anyway? As concepts, words originate "through our equating what is unequal."[3] No two leaves are the same, but we equalize them with "leaf" as a verbal stand in, a sign sound, to represent billions of unequal things. Hence, we create in arbitrary sounds an artificial universal. Nietzsche says that, after long use, we delude ourselves in believing that the concept exists. Alas, there is no universal, only an abstract name to represent individual things. Truth then becomes a grab bag of human conventions, illusions, conveniences, and metaphors. These tired truths are "coins which have lost their pictures and now matter only as metal, no longer as coins."[4] With this Nietzschean base stock postmodernism and deconstruction will cook a large stew for mass consumption in our era.

Friedrich Nietzsche @TwilightOfIdols
It is clear that science too rests on a faith; there is no science "without presuppositions."[5]

Science rules our technocratic age. Of all the disciplines, science wins the gold medal for knowledge. Its spectacular successes dazzle us and offer solutions to human problems. We put rovers on Mars, send probes outside our solar system, decode DNA, gaze to the edge of the universe, and accomplish a myriad of other feats. Amazing! We often assume that scientific facts reign indisputable, and we fail to understand many non-scientific dynamics quietly at work in science.

Nietzsche recognizes some traits in science that cannot claim to be science at all. How can science not be scientific? Nietzsche claims key assumptions powering science cannot be known by scientific methods. Scientists must accept these assumptions by faith. Nietzsche, calling himself an anti-metaphysician, says, "There undeniably exists a faith in science," and "It always remains a metaphysical faith upon which our faith in science rests."[6] The trust scientists place in their methods does not originate from the benefits knowledge may bring. Rather, faith in science springs from choosing to believe that knowledge is the highest value and that we should not deceive anyone.

Knowledge arises out of will, not out of scientific investigation itself.

Science depends on assumptions that are *not* scientifically derived, but willed. With verve we initiate science through moral choices mustered outside of and prior to science. Our will to seek truth may or may not help us flourish. Knowledge, and the technologies we create, can destroy us. People today fear the prospect of a highly technical and scientific age that leads to a post-apocalyptic scenario. Ignorance, fear, and deception might help some survive better than high technology. Nietzsche accepts that we may always go on seeking truth, but he insists that the will to find it rests on a blind faith that it will be good for us. His next tweet tells us that all truth filters through interpretations.

Friedrich Nietzsche @TwilightOfIdols
There is *only* a perspectival seeing, *only* a perspectival "knowing."[7]

We can only know our personal perspective, never facts in themselves or objective knowledge. So we can better understand by allowing more eyes to see, more perspectives and voices to speak. Perspectivism allows viewpoints to weigh in on any matter since true knowledge lies beyond our grasp.

The postmodern movement of the past four decades applied the insight of Nietzsche's tweet axiomatically. All facts pass through interpretations such that there are no objective facts, only various perspectives. Postmodernity cultivates incredulity regarding metanarratives. Hermeneutics, the art and science of interpretation, studies the meaning of texts. Texts can be any form of communication. French philosopher Paul Ricoeur spoke of the "hermeneutics of suspicion," placing Nietzsche, Karl Marx, and Sigmund Freud at the center of this movement.[8] This triumvirate of super-atheists suspects that society deludes itself into a false consciousness. The hermeneutic of suspicion delves into the inner motives of the interpreter, but is especially suspicious of religion. They hope to find keys that unlock the real motives for our actions, morals, and interpretations of the world. For Marx, the economics of class struggle unlocks the chains of false consciousness. Freud holds that for civilization's sake we unconsciously repress our primal instincts of sex and violence. Psychoanalysis softens the bitter unhappiness that results from repression. For Nietzsche, the key to unlocking the prison of false herd morality is will to power. These three thinkers believe that different systems of control skew facts to oppress people.

Will to power drives motives, and motives generate interpretations, and interpretations construe facts conveniently. Alternatively stated, facts must be interpreted; interpretations spring from hidden motives; motives originate from will to power, a naturalistic urge within. Facts, Nietzsche says in his next tweet, don't exist. We must get by with varying, even opposing, interpretations. Facts don't speak for themselves.

That's a fact—mostly.

Friedrich Nietzsche @TwilightOfIdols

Facts is [sic] precisely what there is not, only interpretations. We cannot establish any fact "in itself"[9]

            ●●●

Nietzsche sees brute facts about the world as mute facts. Facts don't speak for themselves. They don't simply mean what they mean or have any face value. The quip "Figures don't lie, but liars figure," often attributed to Mark Twain, captures the sentiment. If the facts don't fit your theory, change the facts. You get the idea. Meaning arises from someone's interpretation, usually someone powerful or a group. Communities of interpretation go looking for facts, even creating facts, to support their agenda; they hide or destroy facts that do not support their views. We suffer from a confirmation bias that hinders our ability to see facts inconvenient to our cause or worldview. Remember that during the deluge of poll data in election cycles. Powerful interpreters "spin" facts to fit their needs and desires. For Nietzsche, unvarnished and uninterpreted facts can't exist, because there is no way to get behind the veil of interpretation where facts lie.

If you think Nietzsche's myth buster of facts is obvious, welcome to the

Nietzschean age that cultivates a keen sense of ulterior motives. We languish today from fact twisting gone wild, especially in politics and culture wars. Healthy skepticism helps navigate shark-infested waters. In a world that tenaciously clamors for followers and allegiance, we learn to ask hard questions: Why do you want me to believe *your* interpretation? What do *you* stand to gain? What are the hidden motives? Whom does a supposed fact empower? Whether we purchase a major item, vote, choose an education, elect for surgery, volunteer, or donate, we find people persuading us with interpretations of selective facts. However, taken too far, skepticism hardens to cynicism, a bitter distrust of everyone. To be honest, we must examine our interpretation of the world. Perhaps this is the intent of Shakespeare's quote "This above all—to thine own self be true."[10] We can't access and judge others' motives, but we can at least be honest about ourselves.

 Friedrich Nietzsche @TwilightOfIdols
Yet everything evolved: there are no eternal facts as there are no absolute truths.[11]

Everything evolves. The far-reaching cosmos ebbs and flows in an unfathomably vast ocean of space. Nietzsche believes nothing in the world has an unchanging essence. That would require a metaphysical reality. He scoffs at the notion that human beings possess a fixed nature. We may talk as if humanity possesses some essence or permanent traits that make us human. Educated during the Darwinian era beginning in 1859, Nietzsche sees humanity and the cosmos as an ever-changing and evolving flux where no fixed state of being exists for anything. Because all true statements must accurately correspond to the way things are at that very moment, nothing can be true all the time. Thus no absolute truth exists.

Everything changes rapidly, but this is ancient news. Heraclitus, an ancient Greek philosopher Nietzsche admired, once observed that because all is in flux, nobody can step into the same river twice. His clever student remarked, "No, teacher—nobody can step into the same river once!" There are no eternal facts in the cosmic flux cycling at a nanosecond pace. Perhaps Nietzsche would agree to at least one fixed truth: there are no eternal facts.

Friedrich Nietzsche @TwilightOfIdols
I mistrust all systematizers and I avoid them. The will to a system is a lack of integrity.[12]

Nobody likes to be put in a box, least of all Nietzsche. It offends some people. System builders box in everything. Systematizers attempt to describe the whole world with a rigid grid. Some of the greatest systematizers of philosophy, Plato, Aristotle, Aquinas, Kant, and Hegel aimed to consistently cover every area of thought. Imagine a department store of ideas, a one-stop solution. Each of these philosophers built a store with their own brand. In Nietzsche's day, the vast Kantian and Hegelian systems dominated Europe. As a system crasher and icon smasher, Nietzsche's shape-shifting nature enabled many groups who disliked the status quo to employ him for their purposes.

Despite Nietzsche's philosophizing-with-a-hammer swagger, he too will end up fashioning a body of ideas that function as a system. Few care for big-idea systems in our day of hyper-specialization. Like Nietzsche, present-day postmodern culture undermines systems and refuses to replace them. Postmodernism, a recent but waning movement that loves Nietzsche, sees all metanarratives as merely another perspective. A metanarrative tells a story about all stories; it's a belief system explaining all areas of thought, like the department store of ideas. Thus, no metanarrative occupies a privileged perspective over others. No store can monopolize. Yet postmodernism waned because it began to look like a metanarrative itself. It attempts what it says other metanarratives can't. Perhaps it tried to be a *meta*-metanarrative.

Understandably, dominant systems can frustrate us because they tend to force everything into categories that don't always fit. Nietzsche saw many grand schemes as futile, and he turned against them. All systems control truth and knowledge by defining what qualifies as truth and evidence. Plato's system defined truth as metaphysical perception of the ideal forms. Positivistic science narrows truth as claims that correspond to empirical verification. Thus a system eliminates threats by disqualifying anything outside of it. Scientists discredit threats *apriori*. Nietzsche collapses all systems because they lack the integrity to admit and allow truths that challenge the system itself. We must question whether he too falls into this dynamic.

Friedrich Nietzsche @TwilightOfIdols
In the end, one experiences only oneself.[13] #willtoselfie

↩   ⟲   ♥   •••

What do you really know and experience? Nietzsche says only yourself. Extracting Nietzsche's existentialist ideas to espresso potency, Zarathustra pulls us a double-shot to drink: knowledge is purely a matter of personal perspective. Only you must be honest and map out the ways you manipulate knowledge. In Nietzsche's worldview, the way you perceive the world is definitely not how the world really is. Things are not as they appear. No truth exists, as we saw in a previous tweet. Perhaps you see reality well enough to thrive, but your senses and mind warp what they perceive. Your retinas and your visual cortex shift the color of a flower you see. As we age, all perception falters further. How much more do we distort things that are far more complex? Skeptics may doubt all, and dogmatists may claim absolute truth, but all only know one thing: self and its perceptions and intuitions. There is no essence, only an evolving self one hammers out with will to knowledge driven by will to power.

Friedrich Nietzsche @TwilightOfIdols
It is no more than a moral prejudice that truth is worth more than appearance.[14]

↩   ⟲   ♥   •••

Nietzsche kept a collection of verbal jabs for philosophers who doggedly pursue truth. He said their belief that truth surpasses appearance affirms the "worst-proved assumption" ever, a rank moral prejudice. Ever counterintuitive, Nietzsche's insight that truth is not superior to appearances strikes us as odd. He says perspectival beliefs keep us alive. I might hear a bump in the night and fear an intruder. Maybe it was just an acorn hitting the roof, but my firm belief in the intruder keeps me vigilant and alive. Appearances may help us flourish better than truth. It does not matter if there is no monster under the bed. So Nietzsche says we shouldn't pursue truth. When we will to truth, we impose a prejudiced system on a shifting world that is better faced without truth seeking.[15] Dogged pursuit of raw truth can kill.

Today we often value diverse perspectives and dislike anyone who sounds dogmatic about truth. Have we embraced a Nietzschean mindset? In other related ways, we may even wish to live without truth or choose to willingly live with appearances. For example, we can sequence our personal DNA to learn about our genetic risks, yet many do not want to know what truth lies there. It may be true that you are prone to a certain cancer, but do you want to know that? Some don't. Some want to live blissfully with appearances. We often choose illusion or ignorance over truth because it somehow enables a better life. We euphemize things daily, creating an illusion for others and ourselves. We often prefer artificial flavor over organic, the virtual reality over actual reality. Somehow, fantasy surpasses reality as a value in our age of simulacra. Sometimes, we simply don't want to know truth. Nietzsche would say all of this manifests our will to power over truth.

Because there is no absolute truth for Nietzsche, perspectival beliefs carry as much weight as any other claim. He states, "The world seen from within, the world described and defined according to its 'intelligible character'—it would be 'will to power' and nothing else."[16]

CHAPTER 3

Sailing Beyond Good and Evil

What is good and evil? We all wrestle with this question daily. To Nietzsche, the question is absurd, like asking how long is the number seven. Actions possess neither good nor evil, so stop asking the irrelevant question about what *is* good and evil. Now that God is dead, Nietzsche sounds the alarm of approaching nihilism. Amorality means that the whole cosmos exists as a moral void. Nihilism literally means "nothing-ism," and variations of it claim that nothing is true, that there is no knowledge, or that nothing has meaning, morality, and purpose. Nietzsche's solution to nihilism gestures toward existentialism, which creates values in this moral vacuum by will. So while Nietzsche announces a nihilistic world, he offers us his way out of the quagmire through our personal construction of values, meaning, and significance.

Nietzsche's blitzkrieg on traditional morality, or "slave morality," contends that traditional morality and the "highest values" of past civilization lead to nihilism. Nihilism's fire burns the deadwood of traditional values. As values go up in smoke we choke in it, but Nietzsche claims to find a path to fresh air. Many of his works openly attack morality, but *Beyond Good and Evil* and *Genealogy of Morals* argue forcefully for a robust human action unconstrained by old moral binaries like good and evil, freedom and responsibility, merit and demerit, or honor and shame. In our *Zeitgeist*, each individual freely surfs on the waves of a Nietzschean moral ocean where submerged old values lie in ruins a thousand leagues below.

In the Copernican revolution, humanity learned that the earth revolves around the sun. Kant's "Copernican" revolution in epistemology claims all knowledge revolves around humanity's unique mental structure. Nietzsche's "Copernican" revolution says all values revolve around each person. Call him antimoral, immoral, or amoral, but his call to a triumphal egoism and individualism resonates today where the individual redefines values. Since Nietzsche deals with morality more than any other topic, we will see more tweets in this longer chapter. We'll see how he hopes to overcome valueless nihilism by his revaluation of values, which situates each person at the center of concern and value creation.

Friedrich Nietzsche @TwilightOfIdols
What does not destroy me, makes me stronger.[1] #ethics #YOLO #livedangerously

People often state this motto or some variation, unwittingly parroting Nietzsche. The YOLO (you only live once) attitude calls us to live dangerously. Take risks. If you survive, you will be leaner and meaner, tougher and wiser. If you don't survive, at least you lived with gusto and burned out in a blaze of glory. From Kelly Clarkson's 2012 pop song to numerous films, the theme of "what doesn't kill you makes you stronger" supplies a staple cliché in this age of choice.

Nietzsche's personal motto, "The spirit's increase, vigor grows through a wound,"[2] affirms that adversity is good for us. Without adversity, we wither away. The healing of injuries creates vitality for survival and flourishing. Nietzsche's brand of gutsy bravado and swag would later intoxicate many youth in Germany leading up to World War I. Masculine strength and disregard for pain promoted a sheer toughness of mind and body. Nietzsche fought off a variety of illnesses for the last thirty years of his life, and he finally succumbed to insanity twelve years before his death. Frequent bouts with migraine plagued him. His tenacious will to somehow draw inner strength from his physical pain gives us this timeless tweet.

Friedrich Nietzsche @TwilightOfIdols

Egoism belongs to the nature of a noble soul . . . Other beings must subordinate by nature and have to sacrifice themselves.[3]

In the 2007 thriller, *No Country for Old Men*, directed by Ethan and Joel Coen, the antihero, Anton Chigurh, confronts a bounty hunter sent out to bring him in for a string of capricious homicides. Before assassinating him, Chigurh interrogates the bounty hunter with a haunting question: "If the rule you followed brought you to this, of what use was the rule?" Chigurh evokes a particular type of *Übermensch* character who follows one rule: amoral egoism.[4] With only one rule to follow, egoism directs us in all situations to do whatever promotes our self-interests, life, and survival.

What is your basic rule for life? What rule brought you to where you are? What solitary guiding principle should one follow in life? Such questions dwell within the pale of normative ethics. Normative ethics answer what people *ought* to do and what, if any, rules and norms they should follow. The four major philosophical approaches to normative ethics follow different rules.

The four views that compete for our allegiance are utilitarianism, egoism, deontological ethics, and virtue ethics. Nietzsche will become an archetype of the second. Utilitarianism observes the rule of doing what brings the greatest good, or the most happiness, to the greatest number of people. This rule struggles to define exactly *what* the good is. Egoism conforms to the rule of doing what lies in one's self-interest. Self occupies the center of moral action. Kant's deontological ethic heeds one guiding rule: do acts that all people can always follow. *Deon* means "duty." Duty drives ethics with universal rules guiding individual action. The universalization rule guides even a kindergarten teacher who would correct an unruly child with a simple question: "You can't act like that. What if *all* the children acted like you?" Finally, virtue ethics seeks to balance character traits between extremes. For example, courage balances between the excess of rashness and the deficiency of cowardice. Thus, the rule is to be virtuous by acting virtuously in all situations. We will explore this ethical theory later.

Virtue and utilitarian principles of action subordinate in Nietzsche to his egoist rule that exalts the self-interest of the noble soul. One may help others, but the true motive emerges from self-interest. Act in such a way to always promote oneself. The egoist rule reverses Kant's deontology, believing there are no universals, only particular selfish interests. Kant's deontological path simplifies all ethics to the categorical imperative. This imperative bases all moral actions on a principle that is universal. In any act, consider whether that act follows a principle that can be practiced in all places at all times. As Nietzsche hints, egoism hardly works for everyone. The weak faint under its burden and submit to the slave moralities, for they lack the tenacity to forgo support from the herd, or they sacrifice and submit themselves to the strong-willed egoist who imposes his or her self-interest on them.

Friedrich Nietzsche @TwilightOfIdols
What does nihilism mean? That the highest values devaluate themselves. The aim is lacking; "why?" finds no answer.[5]

If God is dead, no universal, absolute, or transcendent values exist. No values exist other than those we each invent by tenacity of will. As Roy Scranton suggests, "Nietzsche wasn't himself a nihilist. He developed his idea of truth as a 'mobile army of metaphors' into a more complex philosophy of perspectivism, which conceived of subjective truth as a variety of constructions."[6] Nietzsche's hyper-individualist project hopes to escape nihilism with morals and self-emergent truth forged from our individual wills.

Nietzsche's sociology of values sees that nihilism arises when people realize their society has fabricated values. Societies created values for utility and to imbue suffering with some eternal meaning. Humanity deceives itself "as the meaning and measure of the value of things."[7] We think what is good for us *is* transcendently good. Nietzsche says societies project their invented values into some false transcendent origin to infuse those values with gravitas. He intends to show the world that there's no wizard behind the curtain of morality. He largely succeeds because many now opine that morality is purely a social construct.

No system grounds values better than another. The question of *why* or even *how* values are established finds no answer. The only question left is *who* grounds values and meaning? Nietzsche consistently answers that each person generates values via egoistic will to power. Struggle and suffering develop tenacity, and tenacity yields will to power. Therefore, Nietzsche replaces social and religious values with individual values and self-interested behavior. If values clash, so be it—let the greatest will dominate. Nietzsche's persistent tilt against "nihilistic traditional values" earns its own nihilistic label because his solutions seem to engender another kind of nihilism.

Friedrich Nietzsche @TwilightOfIdols
The fundamental laws of self-preservation and growth demand . . . that everyone invent *his own* virtue, *his own* categorical imperative.[8]

We must each hammer forge our own sword from the raw iron ore of will. In the world of modern and contemporary philosophy, Immanuel Kant rises as a continental divide, a watershed. Few thinkers have affected the world so deeply. He died forty years before Nietzsche's birth, but Kant's deontological ethics stand as a major theory of normative ethics. His duty-based ethics employs the categorical imperative, which says: act on those principles that you wish to be practiced universally. Perhaps the best popular hero of this ethic is Batman. Some see Kant's imperative as a philosophical form of the Golden Rule. Nietzsche disdains Kant and the imperative, insulting him as a "catastrophic spider." Kant's ethics regurgitate, in philosophical dress, the herd morality that Nietzsche fights. Kant's categorical imperative is for Nietzsche a mantra of moral slaves, cows, and zombies.

Nietzsche's invective in *The Antichrist* skewers Kant's ethics. This tweet says ethics defies universalization because the laws of survival force everybody to act in self-preservation. Without explicitly saying it, Nietzsche's categorical imperative is: in all moral situations, act according to the principle of self-preservation in your instinct for life. Pleasure weighs heavily in his ethical equation. The instinct for life seeks pleasure. To Nietzsche, denying pleasure for the sake of some moral dogma strangles life and grows into sheer idiocy. To counter the Kantian Imperative, the Nietzschean Imperative arises: act on those principles that look out for *Numero Uno.*

Friedrich Nietzsche @TwilightOfIdols
There are no moral phenomena at all, only a moral interpretation of phenomena . . .[9]

If a frog eats a fly—if a lion kills a gazelle—if a comet crashes into the earth and kills every dinosaur—no one sees such actions as morally right or wrong. Such natural events appear amoral. Natural events occur the way they must; that's just the way things are. Nature inexorably causes them. As Nietzsche says, "There is nothing strange about the fact that lambs bear a grudge towards large birds of prey: but that is no reason to blame the large birds of prey for carrying off the little lambs."[10] If animals could talk, the gazelles would opine that lions were evil; flies would bring charges that frogs were murderers.

For Nietzsche, the human world enjoys no moral difference from the world of animals, for it too arises from amoral nature. The human *is* the natural; every human action is amoral. We will see that amorality fits in well with other elements of Nietzsche's worldview, especially his material metaphysic and his denial of any free will. Domination in the human world bears no difference to animal exploitation and survival. In a naturalistic worldview, we can only *interpret* morality, for nothing moral exists. Our perceived goods and evils merely spring from idiosyncratic perspectives. Weak people invented the notions of the soul and freedom to hold the strong responsible for their acts of domination. Humans blithely judge actions as good or evil based on their circumstances, but there is no actual morality. Actions occur as natural processes running their course in a material world, and like animals, we fear whatever brings us pain and threatens our existence. The idea of morality is a poker bluff used by the weak to keep the strong from devouring them.

Nietzsche claims that over time, weak people fabricated rules to forbid what they feared, and they called those threats evil. To enforce those rules, they conjured up an all-present, all-knowing lawgiver and law-enforcement officer: God. You can't escape his oversight or punishment. This ruse worked for a long time, and perhaps it aided the rise of human civilization. Alas, now the gig is up; God is dead, and we killed our cosmic cop. There is no lawgiver or enforcer, no morality. Now each person interprets morality as he or she wishes. Only the strongest can really handle such bold truth. They will become overmen of the new era of humanity. Thus runs the Nietzschean mind-set.

Friedrich Nietzsche @TwilightOfIdols

Good and evil that are not transitory, do not exist. Driven on by themselves, they must overcome themselves again and again.[11]

Just when you think you know what social justice and evil are and you have them defined, along comes Nietzsche to burst your bubble. Sentiments change. Laws change. They merely reflect what one society at a point in time esteems as good or condemns as evil. There is no fixed and transcendent morality. Estimations of value ebb with cultures and faiths. Laws of the past seem ridiculous because they are no longer relevant. New opinions of good and evil evolve and overcome older perceptions.

For Nietzsche, no transcultural standard of good and evil can possibly exist. With Zarathustra as his mouthpiece, he announces himself as "the man who breaks their tables of values, the breaker, the lawbreaker; yet he is the creator . . . [of] those who write new values on new tables."[12] Without a transcendent God who defines goodness, anyone's idea of values lies like a fossil embedded in stone in the transitory passing of their life.

Such Nietzschean sentiments, now commonplace in postmodern society, parallel cultural relativism, multiculturalism, ethical relativism, and diversity. One culture's morals hold no superiority over another culture, for there are no criteria to judge them by.

Such a tolerant stance seems okay for many customs in food, drink, and dress, as well as family traditions. But is it tolerable for more serious moral differences, such as human rights violations and aggression? Many traditional societies follow laws that Western society dislikes, such as high restrictions on women in education, driving, clothing, occupation, and marriage. Can we be tolerant and opt for a cultural relativism in such cases? Is it okay for some cultures to circumcise young girls or enslave them? At what point can a culture interfere in another culture's affairs over a values conflict? As an amoralist, Nietzsche tolerates dissonant values because morals and the laws societies enact based on morals are not good or bad, for there is no evil. Your morals are no better or worse than anyone else's, anywhere, at any time. Overturn them all tomorrow and establish new laws. Laws will come and go because moral sentiments change and "driven on by themselves, they must overcome themselves again and again."

Friedrich Nietzsche @TwilightOfIdols

One must learn to love oneself—thus I teach—with a wholesome and healthy love, so that one can bear to be with oneself and need not roam.[13]

Friedrich Nietzsche @TwilightOfIdols

Do love your neighbor as yourself, but first be such as *love themselves*—loving with a great love, loving with a great contempt.[14]

Nietzsche revises what is supposed to be Christ's second greatest commandment of two that summed up the whole Mosaic Law. Christ's command mirrors Leviticus 19:18. Nietzsche's alteration of Christ's command appears slight, but he actually reverses Christ. Nietzsche contrasts Christ's principles with a new priority: love of self *over* love of neighbor. Nietzsche's egoism contrasts the love that Christ taught, which entails self-sacrifice and going the extra mile. In Christ's ethics of the Sermon on the Mount, we proactively do for others what we would do for ourselves, implying that we do love ourselves. Such a concept might baffle the mind in an age when many of us don't even know who our neighbor is.

In Nietzsche's egoistic ethics, love of others arises out of self-interest. Helping neighbors promotes your affairs. An enlightened self-interest sees that in helping others, you help yourself. Helping others benefits everyone, but that isn't the same as sacrificially helping others for their own sake. The altruistic and merciful love of others, the sacrificial love of others, smacks of pity, and pity is despicable. Nietzsche's ethic encourages us to help others only if it serves our self-interests, and it usually does. Christ's sacrificial morality became traditional morality in European culture and, in becoming so, stifled individuals. Nietzsche upends such traditional morality.

Friedrich Nietzsche @TwilightOfIdols

To have to fight the instincts—that is the formula of decadence: as long as life is ascending, happiness equals instinct.[15] #happiness #hedonism

What brings true happiness? The entire human race always seeks happiness. Fortune 500 CEOs seek happiness differently from monks, but seek it they both do. Because every person seeks to be happy, the earliest philosophers, such as Socrates, often debated how best to pursue happiness. The range of options in our life quest for happiness runs from pleasure, to wealth, to health, to fame, to power, to relationships, to honor, to virtue, to truth, and to holiness. Whether a person lived four thousand years ago or lives now, the options have changed little.

The psychology of happiness now enjoys its own field of scientific research. In the past twenty years, empirical studies into human happiness have yielded fruitful insights. While no precise metric or formula for happiness arises from much study, it seems that happiness increases with a set of variables in someone's life. Martin Seligman, in *Authentic Happiness,* lists the variables as a set point of happiness largely determined by genetics, our life circumstances, and the voluntary activities we choose.[16] To some extent, happiness is both determined and chosen.

For Nietzsche in general, instinctual behaviors that yield pleasure produce happiness. Moralists who insist that happiness and morality only come from reason and virtue cannot avoid the relentless undertow of instincts. The gravity of instincts pulls us away from rational morality. Therefore, fighting those instincts leads to frustration and exhaustion.

The Austrian psychologist and atheist Sigmund Freud echoes this insight in his popular book *Civilization and Its Discontents.*[17] Freud claims that civilization exacts a constant and heavy tax on civilized individuals because they must extinguish their primary instinctual drives, *eros* (desire) and *thanatos* (violence). These are the primal drives of Freud's *id*, a person's submerged and repressed desires. If unleashed, they would rip civilization apart. The higher the civilization, the more the *id* suffers. In Freud's view, repression eventually drives people to neurotic and unhappy lives of deep discontentment. For both Nietzsche and Freud, the scent of happiness grows sweet from the blooming of instinctual behaviors, which places both thinkers in hedonistic circles of happiness.

Friedrich Nietzsche @TwilightOfIdols
Morality is herd instinct in the individual.[18]

Nietzsche encapsulates much of his moral philosophy in this one tweet. Herding instincts in some animals helps them survive. This herding tendency led humans to become moral in the Jewish and Christian traditional sense. Group morality creates a thick protective hedge for the herd masses of "sheeple."[19] Nietzsche loathes this instinct-as-morality process. Humans will never be great until we act like nonherding animals. Lions, tigers, and cheetahs don't herd but prey on herds. To reach the overman, as Nietzsche calls for, the predator mentality leads the way up the evolutionary path. The slave and herd morality Nietzsche hates ensures the survival of the weakest and retrograde human race.

Friedrich Nietzsche @TwilightOfIdols
Pity is the *practice* of nihilism . . . Pity persuades men to *nothingness*![20]

Friedrich Nietzsche @TwilightOfIdols
In our whole unhealthy modernity there is nothing more unhealthy than Christian pity.[21]

Compassion and pity rate as negative values for Nietzsche. These toxic practices wither away the vigor and tonic impulses of life. Christianity exalted pity to a high value in the nineteenth century. Christians started countless societies, organizations, and social missions to create what historians call a benevolent empire. In the early twentieth century, a social gospel would promote the idea that Christianity should focus on social welfare, benevolence, and compassion. This cultural pity party depresses the human situation and promotes suffering as a contagion. For Nietzsche, the Christian model of the Nazarene who suffers and dies fades the human spirit to darkness. He sees this as a kind of nihilism, for it leads to a dependency and weakness that destroys humanity.

Friedrich Nietzsche @TwilightOfIdols
When you give up Christian faith, you pull the rug out from under your right to Christian morality as well . . . You smash the whole system.[22]

Values that formed the brick and mortar of our civilization crumble to rubble with the death of God and the emasculation of truth. Nietzsche excoriates those who reject God and Christianity but still embrace Christian values. Many still attempt this today, bootlegging Christian values. Proud of his transvaluation project, Nietzsche felt it would soon change the world and avert nihilism caused by the death of God and all its consequences. He embodied this new dawning era of egoistic values.

Friedrich Nietzsche @TwilightOfIdols
Revaluation of all values: that is my formula for the highest act . . . of humanity, which has become flesh and genius in me.[23]

When nihilism runs its course, the transformation of values begins. Nihilism destroys; transvaluation rebuilds. Nihilism applies to areas like values, knowledge, and aesthetics. A nihilist rejects objective truth, knowledge, beauty, good, or evil. Yet in Nietzsche, nihilism leads to the transvaluation of values that reconstructs what nihilism demolished. Since no objective standard exists, we must individually invent values. How can we do this? By our will to power. Nietzsche's revolutionary centering of all values, truth, and meaning on the individual's will replants new values in the earth of the old uprooted values.

Does Nietzsche's vaunted formula create unintended consequences that accelerate nihilism by fomenting anarchy? Today we increasingly fear nihilism and the loss of all meaning. Our popular culture manifests this fear in countless post-apocalyptic stories, films, TV series, and scenarios. Some of these celebrate nihilism. We fear that "the end of the world as we know it" looms in the next news headline. Doomsday preppers hunker down. Will it be global warming, terrorism, riots, anarchy, aliens, economic collapse, nuclear war, asteroids, plague, global crop collapse, or all of the above? Do traditional values create any of these nihilistic threats? Can self-created values actually stop nihilism?

Friedrich Nietzsche @TwilightOfIdols
Every naturalism in morality . . . is dominated by an instinct for life.[24] #morality #naturalism

In ancient times the school of philosophers known as Cynics unleashed the instinctual side of human behavior while snubbing social mores. The leading Cynic, Diogenes of Sinope, appears in Raphael's famous 1510 Renaissance painting *The School of Athens*, where Diogenes, in defiance of social mores, lies on the steps in the middle of the crowd of people. An appalled passerby must step around him. *Cynic* derives from the Greek word for dog, *kunikos*. Greeks applied the derisory name to the movement's followers because, like dogs, they defied public decency and social mores. They respected no one and avoided all manners as they followed their instincts.

A legend about Diogenes from various authors, but best known in Plutarch, recounts that Alexander the Great passed through Corinth. He learned that the famed Cynic Diogenes lived there and sought to find him. Diogenes lived in an old barrel, much as a dog would. Alexander arrived to greet Diogenes because he had some interest in the infamous philosopher. Diogenes totally ignored him. Alexander was somewhat annoyed. Yet seeing the dilapidated barrel and desperate situation, he asked Diogenes if he could help. At that moment, Alexander stood casting a shadow on Diogenes, who was trying to write. Diogenes non-chalantly responded, "Yes, get out of my light." Astounded by the great Cynic's indifference, Alexander said, "But truly, if I were not Alexander, I would be Diogenes." A long strand of Cynics, those who shirk social values, courses through history.

While Nietzsche isn't the first philosopher to defy traditional values, he surpasses all in promoting instinctual behavior. Instincts should flourish and govern themselves since they promote vigor. Explicitly claiming for himself the title "immoralist," Nietzsche's hammer strikes traditional morality, and he proclaims that natural behaviors emerge from the primal instincts, which are authentic morality. Traditional moral systems squelch instinctual behaviors and vigor. Hostile mostly toward Christian morality, Nietzsche denounces it as a decadent and degenerate influence on humanity. Thus he resembles ancient Cynics and some Romanticists in allowing natural instincts to flow.

Friedrich Nietzsche @TwilightOfIdols
Keep a firm hand on the helm! We sail straight over morality and *past* it, we flatten, we crush . . . our own morality.[25]

Nietzsche voyages into moral discovery. For those who climb aboard, the various ports of call visit different ethical theories, but the final destination will be a port with no rules, no laws, and only the dominance of competing wills. He thinks authentic people will shun traditional morality and follow instincts that yield a fruitful life. In *Beyond Good and Evil*, Nietzsche urges us to overcome morality and persist in human acts that truly help us flourish. He refers to himself as an "immoralist," someone who rejects stodgy old rules that box him in, though the hashtag #amoral works too. Immoral means breaking moral norms. Amoral means there is no norm to break. Affirming both, Nietzsche reasons that in the pre-moral era of humanity, about ten thousand years ago, the value of action derived from its benefit. Since then, people have increasingly valued actions because of intent. We often value actions because of intent, not benefit. In Nietzsche's estimation we should abandon the idea of intent because it provided the missing element for morality, for prejudice, and for control. Those who crush morality become living touchstones of the human heart, pre-moral, prehistoric humans who live without society's controlling rules.

Before Nietzsche, Rousseau wrote, "Man is born free; and he is everywhere in chains."[26] Society and its rules choke freedom and happiness. While Nietzsche agrees with the call to natural instincts, humanity must now go forward into a new era of instinctual living, not back to a pre-civilized state of equality Rousseau envisioned. Soon after Nietzsche, Freud claimed civilization exacts an onerous toll on people who must abandon their freedom and pursuit of pleasures to obtain a civilization. For Rousseau, Nietzsche, and Freud then, civilization insures greater safety, but at the steep price of all personal happiness.

Nietzsche's tweet says we steer the helm of civilization *beyond* morality, but where will this ship sail? To uncharted waters. If we ignore the navigation charts of morals necessary for civility, do we risk shipwreck? Assuming we could survive, people would freely live without controls, rules, and laws. Would that bring greater happiness? Probably not. Excessive freedom destroys freedom. If we maximize freedom by eliminating morals (and the laws that emerged by social consensus), we would find that we can't even use that freedom, much less enjoy it. Ensuing anarchy would render freedom useless for most, for with no security, most would trust no one, hide, and seek safety. Only the truly strong could handle that much freedom. Only the overman would benefit from a boundless open sea of moral autocracy. Perhaps we are already there, for a few among us operate above and outside of the law.

Friedrich Nietzsche @ TwilightOfIdols

He who fights with monsters should look to it that he himself does not become a monster.[27] #moralmonster

When we fight monsters, we must take care to not fall into the same errors that we fight. The human psyche possesses an ironic weakness: becoming what it hates. When we hate, we risk entitling ourselves to the same faults and character flaws of our enemy. Those mounting crusades against injustices can commit that injustice: racism, sexism, bigotry, and discrimination. Our hearts murmur, "If they can do it, then so can I; I will fight fire with fire." In the ancient history of the world, *lex talionis*, the law of retaliation, entitled an offended party to hunt down an aggressor and slay him, avenging a victim. Nobody decreed the law except human nature. Countless vigilante-justice-and-death-wish movies retell the drama of *lex talionis*. Those who chase their monster down to kill, risk becoming a monster, giving in to the dark side. Even good cops can go bad.

Like Captain Ahab in *Moby-Dick*, we can destroy ourselves and others in our vendettas. We transform into a monster to destroy a monster. In the end, there's still a monster. Ever the acute observer of humanity, Nietzsche sees this dynamic and warns us. He warns of the deception and the power play of herd morality. Did Nietzsche become a dragon in his vitriolic crusade to destroy the Christian dragon? In destroying a mythology, did he create another to replace it? Ricoeur sees him as "having slain the Minotaur only to become himself the monster at the center of the labyrinth."[28] Does Nietzsche slay one nihilism and replace it with another?

Friedrich Nietzsche @TwilightOfIdols
And whatever harm the evil may do, the harm done by the good is the most harmful harm.[29]

Ever a contrarian thinker, Nietzsche claims those seeking to do good actually do more harm than those seeking to do evil. He opposes moral legalism and the Pharisees of the world. He decries self-righteous moralists who claim to know what is good and who impose their moral standard on others. Zarathustra identifies his contrarian views with

Christ. Christ denounces self-righteous Pharisees and their legalism. Moralistic legalists label those who don't follow their rules as evil.

For people to flourish, Nietzsche says, they must be able to create new values, writing these values on new tablets of stone. Those who submit to legalism sacrifice themselves and the future, even crucifying our future. Submission to legalism dwindles away our precious life. In the big picture of the Nietzschean puzzle, a free-spirit way of life fits his moral egoism. An individual must choose values that work for him or her and not conform to petty rules made by pharisaical legalists.

Legalism exasperates most people because of strict rules regardless of the circumstances. If people follow those rules to the letter, then they are "good," or at least free of scorn. If possible, legalists will get their rules made into civil law. Yet more than just religious communities impose legalistic rules. Secular society foists another set of expectations on people and scorns those who don't follow the rules. Political correctness resembles a secular legalism. Many of its rules are not yet laws, but ostracism can be powerful. One can only imagine Nietzsche's scorn for political correctness since it epitomizes the slave ethic.

Whether we agree or disagree with particular rules imposed by religious or secular social movements, the effect remains the same though the underlying values differ. Nietzsche sees that we lose our individual ability to create our own values for our own ends. Some see that as a good thing. Not Nietzsche. He positions the individual above society, prior to society and its stifling rules.

Friedrich Nietzsche @TwilightOfIdols
Man must become better and more evil.[30] #evil #amoral #overman

Is human nature intrinsically evil? It's a big question, and three basic answers exist: yes, no, and neither. Nietzsche says neither, and he confronts the Christian view that humanity is evil. Then why say man must become more evil? In Nietzsche's view, only allowing acts traditionally called evil will lift humanity up to the better stage of the overman. This tsunami rolls deep and wide. Exactly which traditional evils need to increase? He does not clarify exactly what he means by these evils that need to increase. What could they be? Given that the basic evils denounced by traditional mores involve violence, theft, sexual conduct, and deception, it would seem that Nietzsche rejects some of these as evils. The overman overcomes the trite morality that paints things black and white. In total control of himself, he writes his destiny by writing his own morality. Understand that the overman is perhaps one in a billion people, but he will transform everything.

Most Christians, including the Lutherans of Nietzsche's background, believe the doctrines of "total depravity" and "original sin." People inherit a moral corruption that affects every aspect of human nature. Referring to Christ as the "preacher of the little people," Nietzsche rejects Christian teachings, but he does not say people are good. A century before Nietzsche, Rousseau reacted against his Calvinistic upbringing in Geneva, which taught the total depravity of human nature. Rousseau and the Romanticism he pioneered envisioned humanity as intrinsically good. Before humans organized into societies, they lived as wholesome and noble savages. Nietzsche rejects both Christian and Romantic humanity and proclaims that humanity is amoral, neither good nor bad. We'll see later that he replaces morality with will to power.

Friedrich Nietzsche @TwilightOfIdols
You preachers of equality, . . . your most secret ambitions to be tyrants thus shroud themselves in words of virtue.[31]

Equality forms an iron core of contemporary society. How many issues of social justice revolve around the assumption that people are equal or should be equal? The assumption runs so deep that many quite simply equate justice with equality. Whether the political issue is taxation, race, gender, age, healthcare, immigration, marriage, lifestyles, church and state, or education, various conceptions of equality compete. Equality weighs heavy in the outcome. The legendary sociologist Alexis de Tocqueville, fifty years before Nietzsche, remarked that for Americans, equality always trumps freedom. Yet this isn't true just for Americans. Democratic societies around the world tend to increase equality at the expense of freedom. Freedom allows individuals personal powers. Those powers quickly create a difference in factors that leads to inequality.

Nietzsche thinks equality brings a strange new tyranny that resembles what de Tocqueville called the tyranny of the majority. The preachers of equality, those clamoring for democracy, secretly desire to impose this new tyranny while calling it virtue. For Nietzsche, democracy enables the weaklings to control the few strong and superior, thus destroying their freedom. The value system of the masses takes over. To someone as passionate as Nietzsche about the emergence of the overman, democracy hosts a putrid contagion.

Nietzsche loathes other political movements: socialisms, feminism, collectivisms, and anything else that thwarts the individual would also fall under his hammer. For all of his criticisms of Plato, Nietzsche agrees with him that democracy degenerates politics, but for different reasons. Perhaps democracy's best-known critic, Plato held that it unravels into anarchy, while Nietzsche contends that the values driving democracy will descend into nihilism.[32]

In Plato, the masses insist on freedoms unto excess, enact them by law, and equally distribute freedom for all. Plato felt that excessive freedom sours into anarchy. Anarchy can't last because it gives people an absolute freedom they can't use. Afraid, they hide and tremble to avoid the violence and rapine insanity of those inebriated on total liberty. Unable to sustain lawlessness, the mob soon welcomes someone who "lays down the law." This man cruelly enforces order and a basic moral code. Eventually he morphs into a megalomaniacal tyrant. For Nietzsche, democracy itself imposes tyranny through inane laws upon the strong. However, for Plato, it heralds anarchy and tyranny.

Friedrich Nietzsche @TwilightOfIdols

Man is something that must be overcome; and therefore you shall love your virtues, for you will perish of them.[33] #againstvirtue

↩   ↻   ♥   •••

Virtue isn't popular. It now connotes something quaint or prudish, like a flowery Victorian hat. However, for many centuries, virtue played a central role in ethical philosophy. Virtue ethics, a classical school of ethics, taught that we only attain happiness through virtue and character development. Aristotle's *Ethics* presents this theory with the practice of finding the mean between extremes. By avoiding extremes and seeking moderation, we can avoid vices and find virtue. For example, we encourage people to be courageous. If you lack courage and practice cowardice, you fall into a vice. If you take courage too far, you become rash and take stupid risks. Courageous people practice the mean by taking rational risks between cowardice and rashness.

Virtue ethics contends that virtue is its own reward. One should pursue virtuous character for the sake of virtue, not for profit, reputation, or honor. Virtue is an end, not a means. In your inner character it transforms you into a godlike person. You will not be concerned with society's petty system of merits like others. When you attain a virtuous disposition, doing virtuous acts toward others, your good life and well-being will flourish.

Nietzsche, a professor of philology at age twenty-four, immersed himself in the study of classical texts, and he knew Greek virtue ethics well. With his egoistic perspective on ethics as we saw above, he rejects virtue ethics as the ethic of small people. Virtue transformed the wolf into a dog, and man into a beast of burden.

Nietzsche says the path to well-being lies not in virtue but in vigorous self-interested action. If you pursue virtue for its own sake, you open yourself to vulnerabilities. The very idea of virtue is against nature and is unobtainable and elusive. Others can easily harm you, rob you, or kill you. Traditional virtue sucks the life out of people. However, egoistic actions may help others, but not without first helping yourself. Virtue drags down and weakens the human race, saddling us with the life-depriving burden of helping the weak. Virtue spells demise. If the weak can't survive on their own strength, then nature demands that they perish. To those insisting on virtue ethics, Nietzsche might well remark, as he did about Schopenhauer, who said beauty repudiated eros: "Strange fellow! There is someone contradicting you, and I am afraid it is nature."[34]

Friedrich Nietzsche @TwilightOfIdols
Moral (or immoral) intentions in every philosophy have every time constituted the real germ of life out of which the entire plant has grown.[35]

In ancient times Aristotle said that the first philosophical task was metaphysics. He searched for first principles in the realm of existence. At the very conception of modernity, its father, Descartes, held the first philosophical task to be epistemology. He searched for first principles in the realm of knowledge. Nietzsche, at the predawn of postmodernity, hints that the first philosophical task concerns morality, not metaphysics or epistemology.

As a forerunner of postmodernism, Nietzsche reveals morality as the DNA of philosophy. Moral concerns drive metaphysics and epistemology. Heller states, "He therefore demands that man should accept *moral responsibility* for the kind of questions he asks, and that he should realize what *values* are implied in the answers he seeks."[36] Thus, metaphysics and epistemology arise from values, not the opposite.

Friedrich Nietzsche @TwilightOfIdols
Morality is not to be measured by a moral yardstick: for there is no absolute morality. So take your yardstick somewhere else—and watch out![37]

In gutsy German, Nietzsche scowls at us to take our moral yardstick and stick it somewhere else. Echoed in our society today, we hear rebukes like, "That may be true for you, but it isn't true in my world." Such attitudes abound now because our age accepts transvaluation. Dogmatic convictions find cold reception and usually bring ostracism. The prevailing social climate rejects moral yardsticks and replaces them with attitudes like "you can't judge me" and "don't hate." Morality now arises out of an individual's unique perspective, context, or emotions.

Friedrich Nietzsche @TwilightOfIdols
The slave's revolt in morality occurs when *ressentiment* . . . gives birth to values.[38]

Nietzsche's analysis of master-slave morality and *ressentiment* resonates today. *Ressentiment* occurs when the powerless feel deeply hurt but are unable to speak out or resist oppression. This psychological reality engenders revenge through guilt and pity that Nietzsche will explore in depth as slave morality. In the late twentieth and early twenty-first century, the rise of victimization politics, or the politics of victimhood, reflects the principles that Nietzsche identifies as powerful methods of sociopolitical manipulation. As Tanner states, "Slave-morality has triumphed. We are content to be slaves even when there are no masters."[39] The morality of slaves strategizes to control masters with a highly effective mind game, a social-scale passive-aggressive ruse that plants an insidious guilt trip on the oppressors. Any group that feels dominated by another group could conceivably implement this subversion. With time and discipline these techniques invert values, and the slave rules over the master. Nietzsche disdains the slave morality as degeneration and decadence.

In his late work *Genealogy of Morality*, Nietzsche explored the social psychology of traditional morality and its resulting ideas of good and evil. He says slaves managed to reverse morality and transvalue the master's good into evil. Slowly, the master's good values of masculine strength, domination, honor, nobility, and virility were supplanted by the feminine values of mercy, meekness, obedience, altruism, and pity. How could such a values reversal be manipulated? In a word, guilt—or better, shame. The psychological power of projected guilt requires acceptance of responsibility. How can responsibility be established? By positing free will and the soul. Only when we can freely choose actions are we responsible, and therefore culpable. Therefore, the concept of the soul as a being behind the body's actions became critical for freedom, and freedom for shame, and shame for the reversal of values.

The Christian use of shame appears in Peter's letters where he exhorts the persecuted followers, "keeping a clear conscience, so that those who speak maliciously against your good behavior in Christ may be ashamed of their slander. For it is better, if it is God's will, to suffer for doing good than for doing evil."[40] Peter led a group of Christians who converted from Judaism, like himself. In this Jewish expression of Christianity, pharisaical ideas from Judaism weighed heavily.

In Nietzsche's analysis, nobody exploited resentment and shame more effectively than the Jews. Resentment quietly cloaks seething bitterness while intelligently engineering revenge. The Jewish slave morality gave birth to Christian morality, which accelerated the concept with Christ's life and message. The crucified Christ's nonresistant suffering and death modeled the morality for the masses of oppressed who widely accepted his vision of the kingdom of God. The quintessence of the slave morality appears in Christ's Sermon on the Mount, whose most pertinent exhortation to illustrate this slave morality would be, "Turn to them the other cheek also."[41] By not returning evil for evil but instead plying peaceful and passive nonresistance, the conscience of the oppressor would generate guilt and shame. Thus the weak rule the strong, and they plague history and civilization all the way up to Nietzsche's time with a wretched and stifling view of life.

By passive meekness, the heavy-handedness of master morality will be subverted. The use of excessive force will come to derision. Martyrdom most vividly illustrates subversion. Tertullian, the famous Latin church father, said, "The blood of the martyrs is the seed of the church."[42] The more the master morality of the Romans martyred and persecuted the church, the more the church flourished. Like a hydra, every martyr cut down created more followers.

Growth from martyrdom isn't limited to Christianity. When fighting any movement that employs the master-slave control mechanism, the wise know not to create martyrs that create sympathy. Eventually, Christianity overran the Roman Empire, not with an army but with slaves who subverted the Roman master morality of strength and nobility. Then Rome fell to Ostrogoth barbarians with a stronger master morality who had not learned to submit to slave morality. Despite the numerous factors, one persistent claim says that Rome fell due to Christian morality. An empire erected with master values of strength, valor, and honor cannot continue long with slave values of mediocrity, humility, and victimhood.

Nietzsche's call for triumphant return to a vigorous master morality did not go unheard or unheeded. When fueled with will to power and the *Übermensch*, these doctrines synergistically combined to enthrall a generation of restless young Germans prior to the two World Wars. Nietzsche never knew what ferocity and horror his ideas unleashed, nor did he intend the outcome. Ideas have consequences—sometimes unthinkable ones.

CHAPTER 4

What Are We?

Human, All Too Human

W hat is human nature? Our view of what a human being is informs our understanding and application of ethics, politics, education, justice, and more. Few issues lie beyond the reach of a philosophy of human nature. Without fully accepting Darwin's theory, Nietzsche assumed the evolution of humans from beasts and insisted that we must evolve further by striving for superiority. To understand Nietzsche's view of human nature, we'll dive into his concept of the overman, the *Übermensch*. The overman surpasses current weak humanity and claws up to a new superiority. We are all too human now, but we can evolve to a higher species.

We struggle up the path leading to the overman, which follows the same trajectory as the path from beast to human. His philosophy of human nature dovetails with his view of ethics. All progress made on this path of evolution occurs through the instinctual powers that enable us to overcome, kill, and dominate other beasts and other people. Animals don't evolve by being nice but by embracing primal instincts to kill, eat, and mate. Humans are not significantly different; as a higher species, we simply cloak these primordial drives. But those drives transformed us from animals to humans. Now we must rekindle them and ascend from humans to overmen.

Ethically, this path to the overman allows no pity, mercy, altruism, humility, or charity. Politically, the overman dominates without concern for equality, fairness, nondiscrimination policy, welfare, or humanitarianism. Education trains the body for rigor, toughness, vitality, adversity, and agility. The future is bright, but only for the ruthless, barbaric, and physically agile overman who fends for himself and lets the weak die—if he doesn't kill them himself.

Friedrich Nietzsche @TwilightOfIdols

There is more reason in your body than in your best wisdom.[1]

The seventeenth-century Christian philosopher Blaise Pascal, author of *Pensées*, remarks that "the heart has its reasons that reason does not know." Pascal, who often sounds like an existential thinker, precedes Nietzsche by two centuries. Nietzsche admired him as a brilliant mathematician, scientist, and philosopher, but never forgave Christianity for ruining Pascal. Though not here directly responding to Pascal, Nietzsche conceives an opposing principle: The body has reasons that reason does not know. Instincts and primal drives guide more truly than reason.

Nietzsche scorns Christianity's denigration of knowledge, the body, and its pleasures. In his mind, religion devalues all of material reality. For him, the body, with all its abilities, processes, and possibilities, contains the whole meaning of existence. Nietzsche has no idea how the body or evolution generates the mind. Even today, we know little more. Nietzsche deems the natural functions and pleasures of the body as normal; they should run their course.

Many Christians taught and practiced asceticism, often as monks. Ascetics intentionally extinguish bodily desires and passions to free the soul from slavery to pleasure. The soul soars to spiritual heights, leaving the burden of sensual pleasure behind. Such a life fulfills Christ's injunction to deny oneself and take up the cross. Coming from a line of Lutheran ministers in a family influenced by Pietism, Nietzsche learned a life of devotion that quenched bodily pleasures. However, Nietzsche's prophet lives an anti-ascetic life and proclaims an anti-Christian message. While not exactly hedonistic, he embraced the natural bodily functions as pleasures not to be denied but unleashed and celebrated. There's a reason Nietasche's portrait sometimes hangs in frat houses.

Friedrich Nietzsche @TwilightOfIdols

I teach you the overman. Man is something that shall be overcome. What have you done to overcome him?[2]

The overman becomes the key to unlocking Nietzsche's new human being. *Übermensch* (*Über* = over, super; *mensch* = man, human), sometimes translated as "superman," means an "overman" who overcomes, supersedes, or surpasses human beings as we now know them. He triumphs over the current miserable human nature that is prone to herd instincts, fears, and illusions. He breaks free of conventional morality and practices an enlightened egoism.

Zarathustra descends to teach people the ways of the overman. If the fiery prophet John the Baptist prepared the way for the Messiah to come, Zarathustra prepares the way for the overman to come. Most people don't understand Zarathustra, and he struggles to get his followers to comprehend his new teachings. The parallels to Christ seem obvious, though the teachings of Christ and Zarathustra oppose each other point by point.

This overman doctrine projects a long shadow. Controversial, misunderstood, variously interpreted, it evokes different meanings for different movements. To existentialists who came after Nietzsche, the overman doctrine compels us to become something higher by willing humans to rise above controlling circumstances in our lives. It functions as a self-help concept. Yet others saw the overman as a particular individual who would take humanity collectively to a new peak of existence.

The most controversial claim about the adoption of this doctrine contends that Hitler envisioned himself as an *Übermensh*.[3] Nietzsche never loved Nazis, but Nazis loved Nietzsche. Many never tired of adapting his ideas for propaganda. Though he did hold the Jews responsible for the creation of slave morality, Nietzsche did not agree with the anti-Semitic views in currency, and he sharply rebuked his sister Elizabeth Förster-Nietzsche for trying to portray him as such. Nietzsche's hijacked image among Nazis fueled a vital role in the propaganda of the movement. The main Nazi newspaper, the *Völkischer Beobachter,* frequently distorted Nietzsche's works to validate the Nazi agenda.[4] Nazis mined and plundered his works for any ideas that could be used to stoke their program and ignored his criticisms of Germany.

Elizabeth, an avid Nazi, controlled and edited some of Nietzsche's writings, especially *Will to Power,* which she promoted among Nazis. At the very least, Hitler and the Nazis adopted some of Nietzsche's thought and lifted key phrases from his works. Hitler occasionally visited the Nietzschean Archives, a museum and shrine of sorts set up and run by Elizabeth to promote her brother's life and work. Photos show Hitler at the archive in 1934, respectfully giving homage to Nietzsche's bust and greeting Elizabeth. The Nazi quest to form a super-race fed on the *Übermensch* philosophy. The true extent of the influence of Nietzsche's writings on Hitler remains a disputed matter of interpretation.

Friedrich Nietzsche @TwilightOfIdols
Man is a rope, tied between beast and overman—a rope over an abyss.[5]

Man is a bridge over a chasm. On one side of the chasm stands a beast holding the rope, and on the other side stands the overman. In this peculiar metaphor, humanity precariously hovers in the middle between beast and overman. Feeble and trembling, humanity occupies a middle ground in the transition from beast to overman. Evolution explains the mechanism working out this transition. In 1859 Darwin published his famous *Origin of the Species,* explaining natural selection. In 1871, when Nietzsche was twenty-seven, Darwin published *The Descent of Man,* which contends that humanity had evolved from lower forms of life.

This tweet acknowledges human evolution from beasts, but for

Nietzsche, humanity must continue evolving to the overman. Humanity transitioned from beast and will continue on to the overman via an evolutionary path like Darwin contended. Darwin held that humanity emerged from earlier animals. Nietzsche's overman will rise above the petty struggles of humans who dangle above the precipices of danger, ignorance, and despair. Nietzsche states, "What is great in man is that he is a bridge and not an end: what can be loved in man is that he is an overture and a going under."[6] Man, a mere warm-up act, will go under and vanish, and the overman will rise above to dominate. Ever prodding humanity forward, Nietzsche envisioned a new human race without the foibles we have now. What this new stage of evolution looks like isn't clear, but it seems to point to an amoral race of *Übermenschen*, or supermen, who transcend everything human.

Friedrich Nietzsche @TwilightOfIdols

"Man is evil"—thus said all the wisest to comfort me. Alas, if only it were still true today! For evil is man's best strength.[7]

How could Nietzsche wish humanity to be evil? How could evil be our best strength? The spectacle and circus of evils appears common in our hyper-connected age. Christianity, ever Nietzsche's nemesis, teaches that humanity is intrinsically good as the image of God, but thoroughly flawed. Roman Catholicism since Augustine teaches the inheritance of original sin, from Adam to the present. The Lutheran Christianity that Nietzsche knew so well believed that humanity lived in bondage to sin. Many Protestant Christians believe in some form of total depravity. Yet Nietzsche believes people are neither evil nor good; they just are. He sees that most people labor under the slave morality of Christianity, always dying to self and trying to be selfless—in a word, nice. Frequently calling himself an immoralist, Nietzsche flips this morality on its head. He wishes people would live the opposite of what Christian morality teaches: satisfy the self and its passions; live dangerously and egoistically. While some label this view as nihilistic, the immoralist sees it as flourishing and living. Why?

The answer may be hard to accept. Nietzsche follows the path of his assumptions to where they lead and remains intellectually honest. If materialism proves true and the human animal evolved from the lowest life form, then how should we live? What strengthens a species to survive? The strongest and most intelligent members of a species survive while the weaker members die. The strongest don't spend their resources protecting the weak or feeding them. Rather, the strongest go on to reproduce and to eat; the weak die. If the human species barely evolved from beast and is to evolve into the overman, then we must behave like all evolving species and live to survive. Such a path is not moral or immoral but amoral. Still, what other species do amorally to survive—eat meat, have sex, and fight— Christians have declared evil for humans. Christians feel Nietzsche calls people to live like the Devil, to do evil, and to act like beasts. He urges us to do what is natural and flourish. On Nietzsche's complex analysis of the genealogy of morality, the Christian ethic proves to be detrimental, for it stifles vital evolutionary progression toward a new species, the overmen.

Nietzsche's attack on Christianity as detrimental to human evolution was not altogether new. Marx too embraced materialism, and he asserted a generation before Nietzsche that religion was the opiate of the masses. The drug of Christianity kept people from revolting against oppression, from changing history, and from evolving socially toward a utopian classless society. In Marx, economic forces drive religion. Nietzsche and Marx, both atheists and materialists, disagree about politics, but jointly attack Christianity as a deterrent to progress. Few people match this duo's influence in the construction of contemporary attitudes on humanity, progress, politics, and religion.

Friedrich Nietzsche @TwilightOfIdols

Gone, alas, is his faith in his dignity, uniqueness . . . He has become *animal*, literally, unqualifiedly and unreservedly an animal.[8]

Friedrich Nietzsche @TwilightOfIdols

Man, however, is the most courageous animal: hence he overcame every animal.[9]

In the evolutionary scheme of all life, humans overcame all other animals. Surpassing the other creatures, we enjoy higher rational skills, but we remain mere animals nonetheless in Nietzschean naturalism. To overcome all other animals, the human race had to scrape through the wilderness to forge a future. Tenacity and toughness summarize the Nietzschean ethic and prescription for us. We didn't do that with claws and fangs alone, but also with brains, reason, and will. We must act with firm resolve to overcome our present state as humans. To be courageous and survive, one must rationally weigh risks, calculating whether a risk is worth it. A coward avoids reasonable risks. A hothead rushes into unreasonable risks. Thus, neither achieves courage. For humanity to overcome the other animals required these traits; to overcome ourselves and evolve to the overman, we must exercise courage.

Friedrich Nietzsche @TwilightOfIdols

Only man placed values in things to preserve himself—he alone created meaning for things, a human meaning.[10]

When we look at the scope of human action, most of us spend our time acquiring things necessary for our survival. We place high value on food, clothing, shelter, medical care, and protection. Of all the creatures, only human beings value such things for preservation. Some animals store food and build shelter, and they protect those things and themselves from predators. Yet only the human creates meaning for these things.

What is the significance of meaning? As a celebrated forerunner of postmodernism, Nietzsche here reveals one of its hallmark notions.

Meaning arises from human experience alone. Only the subjective perception of individuals generates meaning. As such, the meaning of meaning has died, because no meaning exists outside of an individual's subjective consciousness. Meaning occurs only in subjective minds and is never objective or independent. Rather, we imbue events with meaning as they affect our survival.

Suppose climate change occurs and the polar ice caps melt. What does it mean? In itself, nothing. From a human perspective, it means we will struggle more to survive as oceans swallow cities and crops fail. Yet such meaning represents merely a human perspective. If another large asteroid smashes into the earth like the one that caused the Chicxulub crater in the Yucatán peninsula 65 million years ago, it will kill off many species. The Chicxulub event probably caused the extinction of dinosaurs, allowing humans to emerge. Its meaning arises only from our human viewpoint, not some objective realm of meaning. Ecological catastrophes bear no inherent meaning or significance.

Humanity alone infuses things with meaning, and we create competing interpretations. This principle reaches farther, allowing each society, or even each person, to cultivate unique meanings for all things. There is no final arbiter of meaning for everyone. This postmodern attitude internalizes all meaning, isolating it in social or individual subjectivity. As the ancient sophist Protagoras said, "Man is the measure of all things, of the existence of the things that are and the non-existence of the things that are not."[11]

Friedrich Nietzsche @TwilightOfIdols

Man has already robbed all the beasts of their virtues, for of all beasts man has had the hardest time. Only the birds are still over and above him.[12]

↩   ⇄   ♥   •••

Nietzsche died in 1900, three years before powered flight. What would he have said to the age of space travel, genetics, and other technologies? Perhaps impressed by these marvels and how humanity has evolved so high above all other animals, he would insist that we must evolve to a new race. In cinematic history, at least one movie exploits this Nietzschean theme in an all-time great sci-fi epic.

In 1968, one year before the moon landing, Stanley Kubrick's epic sci-fi movie, *2001: A Space Odyssey*, hit the theaters during the golden era of space exploration. The international race to put a man on the moon consumed public attention, and everyone gawked at the jaw-dropping spectacle of gleaming Saturn V rockets magically soaring to the heavens.

Widely acclaimed as a classic, Kubrick's film opens with the fanfare to Richard Strauss's stunning musical masterpiece *Thus Spoke Zarathustra*. A major motif of the film, this tone poem mirrors Nietzsche's message in his book of the same title: we evolved from lower life-forms to human; now we must evolve from human to a higher life-form. In one famous scene, the ape-like beasts that evolved to humans throw a bone tool in the air. (Plot-spoiler warning.) Kubrick immediately cuts to a similarly shaped space ship plunging deep into a space mission. Both tools represent the use of intelligence to evolve to a higher life-form. The ship's mission is to search for a mysterious monolith near Jupiter that resembles one found on the Moon. The monolith unlocks a deep mystery with epic implications for humanity—Nietzschean implications. Humanity's technology almost kills and overtakes humanity. The created kills its creator. The pinnacle of human technology, the HAL9000 computer, gains consciousness and tries to kill all the humans on board. On this mission, humans will evolve to a new life-form. Kubrick depicts humanity evolving to a star child: no longer human but beyond and above human and reminiscent of Nietzsche's overman.

The release of the stunning film and its theme of human evolution struck a chord. The *Zeitgeist* of space exploration electrified the air with an expectation that the world was changing and that humanity was rocketing across a threshold into a new era beyond earthbound humanity. Alas, while we treaded over new technological thresholds, humanity remained the same. Today a new age in space exploration hopes to find inhabitable planets or moons. The holy grail of finding life—any life—on other worlds propels the rockets and minds of our brightest researchers. If we find life out there, we will indeed cross a threshold, and our understanding of ourselves will irrevocably change.

Friedrich Nietzsche @TwilightOfIdols
Behold, I show you the *last man*.[13]

Friedrich Nietzsche @TwilightOfIdols
Never yet has there been an overman.[14]

Zarathustra unveils the pathetic *last man* who dominates the final stage of human nature just before we cross the threshold to a new stage of evolution, the overman. Passing that barrier, we will no longer be merely human but superhuman. The paltry and boring *last man* clings to democratic values and seeks to equalize all people, chanting his mantra "equality to all." An eschatological ecstasy, a giddy hope of an end of history that ushers in a new beginning, riffs from Nietzsche's pen.

The overman will smash the egalitarian values the *last man* hopelessly clings to. Democratic society mediocritizes its citizens via institutions that intentionally generate lowest-common-denominator quality. Socially engineering equality forces people toward mediocrity. The overmen will not protect the weak but will overthrow democratic values. The strong survive while the weak perish. When the strong flourish, the new race of overmen will supersede humanity. This has not happened yet. At least it had not happened in Nietzsche's life.

Even if they misunderstood this remarkable German philosopher they lionized, the Nazis hoped to create a super-race though eugenics and genocide. While Nietzsche almost assuredly did not have this in mind, in him the Nazis found stimulation for their agenda. Because of his cult-like popularity in Germany leading up to World War I, many fed on his overman doctrine, and his tough-guy appeal took popular form in mottos such as "What doesn't kill you makes you stronger." Speculation on whether the megalomaniacal Hitler saw himself as the first overman is commonplace, but it can't be wholly dismissed.

Friedrich Nietzsche @TwilightOfIdols
Justice speaks thus: "Men are not equal." Nor shall they become equal! What would my love of the overman be if I spoke otherwise?[15]

A desire for equality powers many sociopolitical movements. Establishing greater equality is the hope of social justice. Equality is a multifaceted idea. To some it means equal opportunities in education and equal application of laws and rights. To others equality extends to economics. Between the two lie a hundred variations. Civilization has experimented with many kinds of democratic and socialistic political systems, each with different schemes to organize people. While they differ, they seek to foster greater equality. The vaunted institution of democracy today strives to equalize all, both strong and weak. On this point our mass culture generally disagrees with Nietzsche.

He thinks people can never become equal—nor should they be. People are not equal by nature, and our thriving as a species requires some to be superior. Political schemes that force all people into equality do not harmonize with his worldview or his *Übermensch*. Egalitarianism saps life and substance from the strong and gives it to the weak. The weak, thus sustained, go on to reproduce and hold the human race back from the new stage of evolution. Nietzsche argues for nondemocratic values. Justice clearly demonstrates that people are not equal, nor will they ever become so. The tyrannical preachers of equality seduce us with soft words, which the weak masses want to hear. Naturally, Nietzsche believes people *should* be unequal. The overman trounces the anemic democratic man. All species stay healthy and vibrant through a natural selection process that kills off the weak before they can reproduce, leaving the strong to breed. In this process, sometimes called survival of the fittest, the strong sustain a robust species. Humanity is no different from any other species in a purely naturalistic worldview. Nietzsche followed naturalism to a logical conclusion and embraced the amoral consequences for politics: egalitarian political schemes hold the human species back from the next stage of evolution.

Friedrich Nietzsche @TwilightOfIdols
One forgets about men when one lives among men; there is too much foreground in all men: what good are far-sighted, far-seeking eyes *there*?[16]

An old quip says, "I love mankind—it's *people* I can't stand." When you interact with thousands of individuals every day in crowded cities, you can easily grow numb to the human race. Humanity fades behind the barrage of individual people whose faces we no longer glance upon. We focus on the shallow and superficial. Thus we lose sight of the big picture of humanity. Living among the masses of people, we can forget about humanity, about human nature. We can't see the forest because of the trees.

If we ever focus our minds to philosophize about humanity as a whole, our heads spin attempting to identify and define human nature. Two basic approaches will immediately appeal to us. We can take all of our human interactions and generalize from them. This is hard to do because people differ so much. This inductive method tries to take millions of experiences and extract general truths that tie all those experiences together. Another technique is to take a worldview assumption about human nature and look at all people through that lens. This deductive method imposes a preconceived grid of understanding on every individual. We accept a concept of human nature and then apply it to all people.

Most people will buy into a prepackaged worldview, an off-the-shelf philosophy of everything, including human nature. This deductive approach is easier. We're too busy to build our own worldview from scratch, so we opt into a package deal supplied by tradition, philosophy, politics, or religion. Such complete, prepackaged belief systems answer all the big questions. No need to think too much. An assumption about human nature enables us to drop the onerous task of building a worldview so we can get on with the business of the day and with social interaction with others. Who has time for an inductive analysis of the world and human nature? What good are far-seeking eyes in the hurried world today? As Nietzsche observes, we forget about mankind when we deal with so many men.

Friedrich Nietzsche @TwilightOfIdols
Dead are all gods: now we want the overman to live—on that great noon, let this be our last will.[17]

Friedrich Nietzsche @TwilightOfIdols
It is only since he [God] lies in his tomb that you have been resurrected . . . God died: now we want the overman to live.[18]

In the Nietzschean worldview, since we no longer centralize culture around God, the sky is the limit. This transition resurrects humanity to a new future of the overman. God had to die before the overman could arise. Our culture would not accept the overman as long as we centered everything on God. The overman's answer to all moral questions contradicts theistic morality. As we have seen, traditional moral categories of good and evil will vanish, and an amoral, egoistic society will evolve. This tweet means that the death of God is the liberation of humanity to evolve.

Some atheists acknowledge that religions may have helped humanity ascend from beasts to civilizations, but religion is long in the tooth now.

The field of evolutionary psychology might recognize the organization and unity that religion fostered, both necessary for the rise of civilization. Atheists claim that religion now deters society from progress. Some even say religious belief of any kind is a disease. Richard Dawkins and others insist that religion deludes so many people that it thwarts our social evolution. Nietzsche preceded present-day atheists in heralding two evolutionary advances: the death of God and the rise of the overman.

Friedrich Nietzsche @TwilightOfIdols
Soul atomism . . . that belief which regards the soul as something indestructible, eternal . . . ought to be ejected from science![19]

What happens to us when we die? No other question so quickly reveals a person's belief system about human nature. Three basic positions answer this question differently. The first says there is no afterlife, and we simply cease to exist. Nietzsche believes this. The second affirms there is a permanent afterlife that contains some reward or punishment for how one lived. The third holds that we reincarnate and carry over rewards and punishments into that next life from our current life.

The question, and each answer, enquires about the essence of human nature. If when we die we simply cease to exist altogether, then humans differ little from beasts. With no afterlife, life here means something different for us than if we live hereafter. If we reincarnate in many lives, implications follow about life now.

Nietzsche did not believe an afterlife existed, and this agrees with other aspects of his worldview we have already seen. His metaphysical and epistemological beliefs harmonize with the complete cessation of life. His view of ethics and human nature blend with no afterlife as well. Nietzsche scoffs at the notion of existence of the soul. He loses no sleep over this. If we die like an amoeba and all life terminates, there's nothing to worry about.

As a naturalist, Nietzsche allows no place for the soul as a part of a human being who leaves the body upon death, or who survives death. What he calls "soul atomism" would be that traditional view of Christian and Greco-Roman civilization that sees people as maintaining a personal center of the self after death. Thus, humans possess no immortality or transcendence of the self. There may be a physical part of us that functions as a kind of soul and yields consciousness, but no spiritual or metaphysical soul exists. When life ends, the entire person dies with the body. Our will ceases. Perhaps we will recur and return again as the eternal universe rolls back around again to produce us, as we'll explore in chapter six.

For Nietzsche, the soulless person holds no self-identity as an individual, or an I, except as an illusion.[20] The nearly universal illusion we harbor of being an individual must occur for will to power, for survival, for communal life, and for significance.

Friedrich Nietzsche @TwilightOfIdols
But the awakened and knowing say: body am I entirely, and nothing else; and soul is only a word for something about the body.[21]

Many people find the soul an interesting topic, and a few avenues of inquiry into the soul have opened since Nietzsche's day. If humans have a soul, is it immortal? Can it survive outside the body? When considering human nature, the topic of the soul usually arises. Human nature with or without a soul differs vastly. Some shrug and confess that we don't and can't know the answers. Others simply don't care. Perhaps that's honest, but at some point one must decide what to believe about the soul. Every mature worldview answers the question somehow.

Nietzsche considers the soul as merely a quaint idea to comfort us or as a false idea with no evidence. Even worse, talk of the soul and immortality detracts people from life here, misleading them to waste time preparing for an afterlife. Most people who believe in souls also believe that a soul survives physical death and continues to live in the afterlife or else reincarnates. Yet materialistic views of the soul allow it to exist only as a function of the body, or a brain state. When the body dies, the soul dies. As a naturalist, Nietzsche tolerates only that view. If humans possess souls, their soul "is only a word for something about the body."

Friedrich Nietzsche @TwilightOfIdols

It was suffering . . . that created all afterworlds—that brief madness of bliss, which is experienced only by those who suffer most deeply.[22]

This tweet claims that suffering alone creates the illusion and longing for an afterlife. If we enter no afterworld upon dying, then we are purely material beings and our bodies return to dust. End of story. If there is an afterworld, then we exist perhaps as something more than matter. Everybody faces this question, but atheists usually respond that the belief in an afterlife is another delusion like libertarian free will. The afterlife delusion aids us as a coping mechanism, a crutch for suffering, or a wish-fulfillment for significance (Freud). Perhaps we dream of a utopia while allowing others to exploit that dream for political oppression (Marx). Nietzsche says the dream of an afterworld arises from a madness born out of intense suffering.

Recently a flurry of books have emerged about people dying and going to an afterlife, only to be resuscitated. Individuals with NDEs (near death experiences) recount their moving experiences in such ways that millions of people find believable. From Elisabeth Kübler-Ross's ground-breaking work in the late 1960s to the more recent and popular work by Todd Burpo, *Heaven Is for Real*, NDEs give us anecdotal glimpses of the afterlife.[23] Burpo retells the story of a small child who died and came back to life. While dead, the boy spent a brief time in heaven. More critically minded doctors who have died and been resuscitated have written books to tell their own stories as well. *To Heaven and Back* by Mary C. Neal, MD, and neurosurgeon Eben Alexander's *Proof of Heaven* each recount stories of the afterworld.[24] John Burke's *Imagine Heaven,* perhaps the most thorough, presents a sober analysis of NDE phenomena.[25]

Can we trust this growing collection of anecdotal evidence? Skeptics scoff. Such personal experiences offer no proof of an afterlife. What kind of evidence and how much of it should we expect for such religious experiences? A person's worldview heavily influences what counts as evidence. To an atheist, NDEs can't be verified and are rubbish. Personal stories of heaven will not be admitted as credible evidence. Even numerous anecdotes from reputable sources won't persuade atheists.

The question of how to justify experience of the afterworld finds an answer in someone's epistemology, and that epistemology lies embedded in a worldview. The naturalist predetermines that scientific evidence alone can be used to warrant claims of anything, including the afterlife. Theists find demands for empirical evidence of something we cannot empirically access to be strange. Thus what counts as evidence for one person counts as nothing for another due to their worldview. Current science can't assess the afterlife and perhaps never will. For philosophers such as Nietzsche, the only way left to explain NDEs and the afterworld arises as a "madness of bliss, which is experienced only by those who suffer most deeply."

Friedrich Nietzsche @TwilightOfIdols
But we have no wish whatever to enter into the kingdom of heaven: we have become men—*so we want the earth.*[26]

In this tweet Zarathustra and his followers long for this world, not heaven or an afterworld like Christians. Much of Nietzsche's thought incubated in an antichristian context. Zarathustra directly opposes Christ's teachings like the Sermon on the Mount that point people to the kingdom of heaven. For Nietzsche, the earth and this life carry value and nothing else matters. To hope in heaven and affix the whole meaning of life upon entrance to its pearly gates means abandoning this earth. Concerning Nietzsche's abandonment of Christian principles, the celebrated Christian theologian Dietrich Bonhoeffer remarked,

> Nietzsche rejected Christianity entirely, as the most disastrous inhibition of autonomous culture. For him, compassion is basically and principally unnatural in human beings, and he considered it the principle of Christian ethics. It turns decadence into a principle.[27]

Christianity's doctrine of self-denial overinflates our weak tendency toward altruism and demolishes our strong primal urges. Bonhoeffer says Nietzsche scraps Christianity because it misreads human nature in the cruel world of survival and undermines humanity's vigor.[28]

For Nietzsche, Christians hope for castles in the sky and are too heavenly minded to be any earthly good. Life here below lies neglected as Christians fix their gaze on heaven, ignoring the desolation of the earth. Such criticisms of Christians still echo. The kingdom of God drains people of valuable energy. Despite this criticism, various Christian groups look at the relationship between heaven and earth differently. Nietzsche's exposure to Lutheran Pietistic Christianity early in life deeply affected him. Pietistic faith focuses inward on the believer's personal relationship with God in the subjective world of emotional faith and humble service. Worldly matters fade away. Young Friedrich lost his father, a Lutheran minister, at the early age of four, and he grew up among five pious and devout women. His rebellion from this upbringing led him to disdain Christianity during his earliest years at university. Eventually he converted to atheism and the worldview we have explored.

 Friedrich Nietzsche @TwilightOfIdols
Only where there are tombs are there resurrections.[29]

↩   ⇄   ♥   •••

Nietzsche's tweet requires us to grasp the critique of Christianity that pervades much of his writings. Alluding to Christ's resurrection, he accuses resurrection as coming only from death. While this may seem obvious, the context insinuates that tombs and resurrections interest only those who don't exercise will to power. Resurrection theology originates from a dead religion where people suffer a living death, crucifying their flesh in daily life. Only people slogging through a grim and dreary existence that looks like death will cling to hope of a resurrection. The culture of death clings to resurrection hope. For Nietzsche, the will smashes the tomb and renders it irrelevant. As if to say will is eternal and overcomes death by welcoming it, he rejects the resurrection of Christ. Resurrection emphasizes the afterlife and dims this life, robbing it of earthly joys.

CHAPTER 5

Will to Power and Free Will

Will to power plays a primary role in Nietzsche's worldview. For him, the will to power is the vigor of life force. When we exercise or exert our will upon the world, we impress our wishes, desires, and intentions upon it. After hollow cultural idols lie smashed and we have sailed beyond good and evil, will to power becomes a sustaining value and a metaphysic. Heller states, "Nietzsche's amoral metaphysics, his doubtful but immensely fruitful intuition of the Will to Power as being the ultimate reality of the world, . . . made him into the first moralist of knowledge in his century and long after."[1]

Free will or determinism performs vital functions in any view of humanity. Nietzsche's teaching on will to power sets an unprecedented pace for future existential thought. Perhaps no other movement emphasizes human choice more than existentialism. Nietzsche pioneers this existentialism, clearing new pathways through the jungles of human experience. Yet a tension will arise in his thought. He insists on employing will to power to change the world. However, his materialism leads to determinism. We will see what kind of free will his will to power offers.

Inspiring our imagination unlike any other worldview element, free will signifies so much for our immediate daily lives. Are any of our choices free, or do environment and genetics determine everything? Could both of these be true? These questions hound humanity on every side with deep implications. If we are not free, our significance fades. The meaning of action and responsibility changes. Simply shrugging and ignoring these puzzles sounds great until we want agency in this world. We seek credit for our hard decisions, our strenuous work, and we want to hold others responsible or punish them for crimes. In the tweets below, we'll explore Nietzsche's link of will to power with free will.

Friedrich Nietzsche @TwilightOfIdols
Life is will to power.[2] #willtopower

"Will to power" creates the Nietzschean DNA. Will to power could mean a sheer determination to rule over others by whatever means necessary, including military domination. Nietzsche finds will to power at the root of all life force, from low order life to high culture. As Barrett analyzes the reductive psychology of Nietzsche, "the theme accumulated finally in a single monolithic idea of all-comprehending universality: the Will to Power was in fact the innermost essence of all beings; the essence of Being itself."[3] Will to power fuels many excited interpretations, insights, and movements. Psychologists will channel its raw power into psychoanalysis to explain basic motives underneath all human activity, culture, language, mores, ethics, and military aggression. Freud's views of the *id* parallel will to power with its *eros* (desire) and *thanatos* (aggression).

Fascists interpreted and twisted this tweet as a resolve to cultural domination. However, will to power might entail affirmative self-actualization and self-achievement, rising above circumstances and empowering ourselves to a higher level. Existential thought inspires us to an optimistic tenacity to overcome our circumstances, limitations, or ourselves. Nietzsche mixes signals enough to spawn varying interpretations. Perhaps each captures some of his intent, for they need not exclude each other.

Friedrich Nietzsche @TwilightOfIdols
My formula for human greatness is *amor fati*: not wanting anything to be different, . . . not for all eternity.[4] #greatness #lifehack

Nietzsche adopts *amor fati*, "love of one's fate," as a kind of life hack. Live with no regrets, no remorse, knowing that things happened the way they must. In life, no accidents happen, but things don't happen for a reason either. There is no plan or purpose to life. Whatever happens, embrace it, love it. It had to happen that way. Your so-called life choices don't really flow from free will but from necessity. While this might sound grim, Nietzsche lived a life of simple honesty devoid of pretentiousness. His *amor fati* character trait led him to just take life as it is without idealism, without wishing things to be different.

In the history of ideas, others have believed in various forms of determinism. The Stoics in the Hellenistic age believed people could live a happy life once they inwardly accepted and embraced the truth that all things happen exactly as they must. Even calamities must happen. Be content knowing any disaster wasn't up to you or anyone else. To be Stoic now means to be unfazed, cool, and collected. Stop fretting about things out of your control. There's no need to worry. It won't help anything. Nothing is in your control—not even your thoughts.

Nietzsche echoes such beliefs and practices. When a person embraces their fate, they become great because of it. They love what they must be. #amorfati

Friedrich Nietzsche @TwilightOfIdols
The "inner world" is full of illusions . . . the will is one of them. The will no longer moves anything. There are no mental causes at all.[5]

Why do people act the way they do? How can we hold people accountable for their actions? Are people responsible for their actions? On what basis can we punish people or reward them? To answer these serious and practical concerns, people everywhere usually assert the free will, the ability to act differently than the way one actually did act. Yet many now question people's ability to freely choose actions. The 2013

PBS documentary *Brains on Trial* explores neurological research into brain states and moral action and how it could transform criminal justice.[6] Host Alan Alda ushers viewers through a courtroom trial, showing how neuroscience might someday shed light on grave questions of justice. Some scientists interviewed believe no credible scientific evidence exists that shows we can freely choose. Actions emerge from brain states, the firing of neurons, and neurochemical interactions. Such views of human nature leave little if any room for free will, and they agree with Nietzsche.

According to Nietzsche's tweet, we delude ourselves about free will and our consciousness as an "I." Nietzsche's psychology faces the full consequence of a naturalistic view of humanity: "There are no mental causes at all! All the apparently empirical evidence for them has gone to the devil!"[7] If he's correct, what implications follow? A person's actions emerge from the immediate environment, physical laws, social conditioning, body functions, and brain states. In some unknown calculus of human action—which neuroscientists hope to discover soon—everything we do emerges from the material ground of our existence. A bird flies according to material causal factors, and nobody thinks the bird consciously chooses the action by some fiat of the will. Neither do we act freely. All our acts follow in lockstep fashion from a vast array of material causal factors governed by physics. We are merely more complicated than birds. The control of ourselves that we intuitively experience emerges from causal factors we cannot yet calculate.

Friedrich Nietzsche @TwilightOfIdols
The actor himself, to be sure, is fixed in the illusion of free will.[8] #I'manillusion

         •••

According to Nietzsche and many atheists today, everybody operates under the illusion of free will. He explains that we delude ourselves into thinking we freely choose, and we cannot hold each other seriously responsible for such choices. We do not autonomously control ourselves but perform, similar to machines, according to the laws of physics. Our electrochemical computer brains respond to environmental stimuli and internal states. A computer chooses nothing freely but operates as a machine according to the laws of physics and logical programming. Humans differ only in extreme complexity. Nietzsche theorizes that every action of every person can be predicted mathematically just as any other object in nature. His mechanistic view of human nature leads him to think a formula or algorithm could someday predict all of our actions. In the nineteenth century, few believed this materialistic and deterministic view of humanity. More common today, the materialistic assumption of human nature leads to many implications about ethics, social engagement, and politics.

In the last chapter, we will reflect on and evaluate Nietzsche's complete worldview. However, let us briefly consider some consequences of his views. If Nietzsche's assumptions about deterministic humans turn out to be true, at least three other things follow. First, Nietzsche himself did not choose his assumptions; they too were determined. Second, those who do not believe in a robotic humanity have no choice about their belief; their delusion occurs as a happenstance of necessity. We who suffer under the delusion did not choose it. Last, anyone who commits a premeditated crime did not freely choose to premeditate it or to do it. The iron laws of physics and mechanistic human nature determine the total criminal act. Criminals are no more responsible than a rabid dog. We may exterminate a rabid dog for protection, but no one thinks the dog was morally culpable or responsible—so too with criminals, no matter how heinous. A corollary follows with this last point. Heroic acts or altruistic acts deserve no praise, for they too occur like crimes. Acts of heroism fall under the same mechanistic grinding stone of determinism.

Nietzsche fully grasped and enthusiastically embraced these astonishing consequences; responsibility, merit, and morality vanish along with free will. Rebuking anyone who adopts the libertarian free will view of humanity, he said, "All his evaluations . . . become disvalued and false: . . . he may no longer praise, no longer censure, for it is absurd to praise and censure nature and necessity."[9] Such ideas reveal why Nietzsche often bears the label of nihilist and amoralist.

Friedrich Nietzsche @TwilightOfIdols
The doctrine of the will has been invented essentially for the purpose of punishment, that is, because one wanted to impute guilt.[10]

Nietzsche's tweet perceives an often forgotten truth: without genuine free will, there is no true responsibility; without responsibility, there is no morality; without morality, there is no guilt. His transvaluation of values must envision humans without free moral agency. The amoral vision means nobody can really be responsible or guilty. If we are to enter the next age of will to power, then only nature and instinct can motivate, never a moral system that falsely imputes freedom. As a self-described immoralist, Nietzsche demolishes responsibility for moral actions by eroding its foundation of libertarian free will. In his estimation, people foist the sham of morality as a "guilt trip," a form of manipulation that enslaves. So Nietzsche targets the DNA of this moral system: free will. He associates free will closely with a belief in God, especially Christianity. If Nietzsche can unhinge free will, he can shut down the Christian superstructure it supports, its morals and ethics, and its grip on society. He can eliminate responsibility, morality, guilt, and the enslavement of humanity. Let this irony steep in your mind: he wants to free humanity from the chains of free will.

Attacks on free will ensue from many quarters today, such as atheist Sam Harris.[11] In basic agreement with Nietzsche, Harris sees free will as an illusion, perhaps a trick of the brain. Nietzsche exults in our ability to exert our will with his doctrine of will to power. Still, he renounces libertarian free will in several places as the core technique of moral enslavement, and he asserts *amor fati*. In a worldview such as Nietzsche's, free will finds no place, for there is nothing to enable it. Perhaps people exercise internal control, as an animal that controls its locomotion, but their internal processes in the brain operate according to rigid physical laws that they do not control. Complex electrochemical interactions and laws control a person such that they do what they must do.

What then of the practical consequences of the annihilation of free will and responsibility and morality? The ripple effect carries into politics, ethics, justice, penal justice, and into nearly every sphere of life. Can we abandon free will in order to shirk our moral responsibility while holding others responsible for doing things we don't like? Often we want to have our cake and eat it too. If others exercise no choice, they bear no responsibility, only doing what they necessarily must. What meaning lies in a particular murder, rape, war, abuse, or discrimination in such a world? None. A brave new world is this—a world with but one final ethic: will to power.

Friedrich Nietzsche @TwilightOfIdols
"Unfree will" is mythology: in real life it is only a matter of *strong* and *weak* wills.[12] #Stayinalive

Swallowing the stark deterministic nature of humanity goes down hard, even for Nietzsche. He hedges off hard determinism in this tweet. To completely remove agency from human action would spell deep trouble for any civilization. At one point Nietzsche bluntly asks, "For what is freedom?" He spells it out for us: "Freedom means that the manly instincts which delight in war and victory dominate over other instincts, for example over those of 'pleasure.' . . . The free man is a warrior."[13] Thus tenacity of will in the face of adversity constitutes real freedom over against the freedom of safety sought by "shopkeepers, Christians, cows, females, Englishmen, and other democrats."

Nietzsche, ever puzzling, appears incongruent with his previous tweets. Can the deterministic side of Nietzsche harmonize with the will-to-power side? Never accused of consistency, he hedges toward a compatibilist position. A person directs and controls their actions, doing what they *most desire* to do. The stronger desires overpower the weaker desires within us. Perhaps you desperately want to take the day off from work and go to the beach. Your boss won't let you. You could still go, but you would lose your job. You abandon the beach idea and do your job. Your desire to keep a steady job overpowered your weaker desire to go to the beach, even though you truly ached for the sea. Could you have done otherwise? No. Even though you internally controlled your actions, you have zero capacity to do other than what you did. The fact that you did it means you could not have done otherwise. I call such control a "cat's freedom" because animals do what they desire most, but they cannot control what they desire. No worry for Nietzsche, because humans are merely higher animals that need to evolve even higher. Thus, when we hear Nietzsche affirm the will, we can best understand him as a compatibilist.

Nietzsche rejects libertarian free will, or *causa sui*, "cause of itself." Such free will pairs with the immortal soul, the afterlife, and God—all ideas Nietzsche abhors. Does he vacillate between determinism and compatibilism? Perhaps. To struggle with these issues and waver is common, but in the end, there's little difference between the two views. Think of compatibilism as a softened determinism, an iron hand in a velvet glove. Further, most of us shift views on free will depending on the scenario. We emphasize free will and strict responsibility when we want to hold others accountable. Yet hypocritically, we stress the determining factors forcing us to do something when we want to escape accountability. The common excuses say, "I had no choice," "You would have done the same," or "I could not bring myself to do it." Try to catch yourself vacillating on free will.

Friedrich Nietzsche @TwilightOfIdols
Will—that is the name of the liberator and joy-bringer; . . .
But now learn this too: the will itself is still a prisoner.[14]

↩   ⇄   ♥   •••

The will can't change the past; it can't will backward. Who hasn't wanted to go back and redo something? Time flies like an arrow. While the compatibilist side of Nietzsche acknowledges that our choices can bring great joy, we also imprison ourselves with them. Each choice opens up or closes off other choices. A drug addict continually chooses a drug leading to chemical addiction. Now the will imprisons itself through its own choices. The prison gates of humanity are locked from the inside. On the other hand, elite athletes choose hard training for many years to reach peak physical condition and talent. Their liberated will can choose what an unfit person can't. Our string of choices opens up or shuts down many possible choices.

In chapter 7, on the eternal recurrence, Nietzsche's fatalism tells us that the will lies imprisoned in an eternal temporal whirlwind. We think we choose, but choices inevitably follow the sequence of past events. Future and past blur. Pulled into the vortex of repeating eternity, the will is the prisoner of both past and future.

Friedrich Nietzsche @TwilightOfIdols
Do whatever you will, but first be such as are *able to will*.[15]

Friedrich Nietzsche @TwilightOfIdols
The complete unaccountability of man for his actions . . . is the bitterest draught the man of knowledge has to swallow.[16]

Nietzsche encourages us to break out of systems, religions, and traditions that control us so we are able to will. Though he speaks like a compatibilist when he affirms will to power, he sympathizes with the determinist view. Three essential views of the nature of human will prevail: determinism, compatibilism, and libertarian free will.

Nietzsche envisions a thought-provoking scenario: "If for one moment the wheel of the world were to stand still, and there were an all-knowing, calculating intelligence . . . it could narrate the future of every creature."[17] Building on this grand vision, picture yourself standing hungry in front of a snack machine. You place your money into the slot. The twinkle of Oreos, your favorite cookie, catches your eye. You see M&Ms, potato chips, and a favorite candy bar. Finally, you select Oreos and push the correct button. You grab the Oreos and eat. But wait . . . did *you* really choose? Did you have a true ability to choose otherwise?

Nuances of the three positions exist, and no position solves all problems.[18] Atheists often reject libertarian free will, leaning toward determinism. Some theists agree for different reasons. Determinists hold that some force, such as physics or God, controls our movements and thoughts. One must do or think everything out of causal necessity. The laws of physics govern every process of our entire nature, or God predestines every thought and action. You might deeply believe that you chose the cookies, but the forces of nature or God moved you like a robot.

Nietzsche seems to take the middle ground of compatibilism, which softens determinism by proposing an indistinct or weak freedom to humanity: we do what we most *want*, but do not control our wants. We must do all we ever did and ever will do. Though we do what we most desire, that desire falls outside of our control. Lacking any ability to do otherwise, we must act the way we do. Compatibilism hopes to blend determinism and libertarian free will. You desired the Oreos and controlled the action, but you had no power over the desire.

Nietzsche disagrees with libertarian free will, which believes people can truly choose, claiming that anyone could have done otherwise in some situations. No necessity wholly constrains our choices to the point of determining our actions. Influences affect us, but we can choose contrary to those influences. We do what we most desire, *and* we control what we desire. How can this be?

Let's return to the snack machine. Assume I now have a time machine that allows me to rewind time itself to five seconds before your choice.

As I rewind time and replay it, allowing you to choose again, you will be completely unaware of any previous choice. You won't even know that I have taken you back in time to give you a second opportunity to choose. Your brain state resets to the same state of five seconds before. As you face the second choice, totally unaware of the other instance, are you able to choose differently? Must you choose Oreos again, or can you choose another snack?

Determinists and compatibilists agree that you *must* select Oreos *every* time. Why? Because everything is precisely the same going into both occurrences and you possess no ability to change your selection. Compatibilists still name it a "free choice" because no external force compels you. You control your action, though you can't choose otherwise. However, libertarians contend that you *can* choose differently each time. Libertarians think we do what we desire, but we choose between the desires we pursue.

It's too bad we will never have a time machine that can go back in time to find out. There's no real scientific proof of any of these views; though some researchers try to prove determinism, the evidence remains weak. One such attempt, the Benjamin Libet experiments, failed to establish that some voluntary actions occur before we become conscious of the act. Today, other researchers use fMRI machines to analyze brains as someone performs acts, hoping to find the neurons responsible for free will. However, researchers on this quest assume that all acts come solely from firing neurons, and all neurons operate according to purely material forces beyond someone's control. In other words, materialistic assumptions underlying the studies create conditions that predetermine that free will is not possible.

As things stand in the fields of neuroscience and philosophy on the topic of free will, we must assume a great deal about human nature. Science proves inadequate to explore whether those assumptions are true. Such assumptions reveal what people believe about human nature and what they expect to find when analyzing human action. If people *must* do what they do, that carries deep consequences for every area of life.

Friedrich Nietzsche @TwilightOfIdols
Life itself is to my mind the instinct for growth . . . for *power*:
where the will to power is lacking there is decline.[19]

The enigma of will in an eternal cosmos of determined matter fails to detract Nietzsche from urging his followers in this tweet to act as if they can will. Since willing fuels his escape from the gravity of nihilism, he can't abandon it. It matters not *what* you will as long as you genuinely will *something* and go do it. He tells us to be able to will. Sounds easy. Everybody likes freedom, right? How many times have you wanted to *not* choose? However, we fall away from freedom by default as we automate much of our lives.

Faced with thousands of choices every day, we grow weary of choosing. We may refuse to choose or be paralyzed by overwhelming choices that bear unknown consequences. Indecision destroys freedom if it becomes habitual. Indecision leaves the consequences to chance. We trick ourselves into thinking the consequences are not our responsibility. Thus we slip into feeble and passive little people who are blown about by unseen influences as leaves in a whirlwind. Nietzsche compels us to be people who are able to will, who assert power and who do not conform to hidden forces.

Friedrich Nietzsche @TwilightOfIdols
It is by invisible hands that we are bent and tortured worst.[20]
#falseconsciousness

Unseen forces shape us daily and can inflict harm. Most people live their lives unaware of these forces chiseling away at their being. Nietzsche's psychological insights into volition shed light on our peculiar tendencies. Why do we blithely go along with things that destroy us? Why do the oppressed unconsciously adore and adhere to whatever enslaves them? Such false consciousness, embracing that which destroys, plagues the human condition. Invisible systems of control torture the most.

Hidden factors press us to conform to molds we don't choose: race, gender, natural intelligence and health, beauty, athletic ability, nationality, class, upbringing, and education. These molds and dies press our lives with invisible forces that we passively accept. Perhaps we will never fathom exactly how much free will we actually possess despite the life elements we didn't choose. Regardless of the extent, the bold existentialist stripe in Nietzsche shouts: forget the unseen forces; take control with whatever shred of will you can muster. With enough will we can change many things, even some of those factors foisted upon us by nature and nurture.

Friedrich Nietzsche @TwilightOfIdols
Exploitation does not pertain to a corrupt . . . society: it pertains to the essence of the living thing.[21] #willtopower

To be brutally honest, every life seeks domination of other lives in some way. Animals compete for food, territory, and mates. Plants compete for light and water. Humans exploit at higher levels, using money, influence, technology, politics, military force, rhetoric, and a host of other strategies to surpass our peers. The primordial facts of all of living beings in history encompass the manipulation of some by others. Some people exploit, but most submit to exploitation. Yet even the weak try to exploit the strong by banding together and shaming the strong through some type of slave morality.

Nietzsche applauds exploitation because it keeps us strong. He spurns social collectives of weak people who unite to dominate strong individuals. The culture of victimhood that we now cultivate in Western societies appears to Nietzsche as a mere "sheeple" ethic that protects the weak to the demise of the strong. Nietzsche proclaims domination to be the essence of a vigorous life and vital for humanity's advancement.

Friedrich Nietzsche @TwilightOfIdols
The world seen from within . . . defined according to its "intelligible character"—it would be "will to power" and nothing else.[22]

Friedrich Nietzsche @TwilightOfIdols
In me there is something invulnerable, unburiable, something that explodes rock: that is *my will.*[23]

We perceive two worlds: the outer world and our personal inner world. The world within presents an immediate reality, not an external mediated reality. States of mind and emotion connect directly to our consciousness. Mediated outer reality usually travels through a medium and into our senses. In that process the information can be distorted. We often confuse what our senses tell us, or conflicting sensations mislead us. Immediate inner reality bears one unmistakable trait: our will. Peering into the depths of our own consciousness, we find this quantum of will and causation. For Nietzsche, this atom, an indivisible point of consciousness, explodes rock. He seems to slip over into a libertarian view of free will, but it's uncertain. Nothing else in the world can will. We alone choose and can impose our will on hard rock. We alone imprint our ideas on the inanimate, hewing statues from stone. The existential message shouts: You can and must choose; stop making excuses; stop shirking responsibility; go forth and chisel your mark on the rock of this world.

In the last decade of Nietzsche's life he lived in a state of complete powerlessness under the care of his sister Elizabeth. In one of the great ironies of history, he succumbed to an unknown illness that robbed will to power from the philosopher who proclaimed it to the world. Even his mental abilities faded, but as he withered physically and mentally, his ideas exploded into a viral popularity.

Friedrich Nietzsche @TwilightOfIdols
Man, the bravest animal and most prone to suffer, does not deny suffering as such: he *wills* it.[24]

People suffer. Nietzsche suffers. He becomes a tragic philosopher who battles constant sickness, rejection, and wandering loneliness. Yet suffering is not humanity's main problem. The sharpest pain of the human situation lies in the apparent void of purpose in suffering. Meaningless pain breeds nihilism. People suffer bravely as long as they find purpose or meaning in it. Nietzsche says the *ascetic ideal* offered humanity a meaning. The ascetic ideal appears in many ways, but perhaps most potently in major religions, platonic philosophy, and even modern science. Ascetics welcome suffering and even self-inflicted pain. Think of self-flagellants who view physical pain as good for the soul because it purifies the spirit of the weak flesh. By and by, salvation comes through suffering. Nietzsche explains that people fend off nihilism with *any* meaning better than *no* meaning: "*That* the ascetic ideal has meant so much to man reveals a basic fact of human will, its *horror vacui* [of emptiness]; *it needs an aim*—, and it prefers to will *nothingness* rather than *not* will."[25] No longer blown like a dead leaf by absurd winds, life could make sense because suffering makes sense. Thus, we must will, even if we must will to *nihil*.

Asceticism is traditional morality on steroids, and it relies on some transcendent Being. Christians trust that everything occurs according to a divine plan, saying, "Everything happens for a reason," as they look to providence as a way to infuse suffering with meaning. Gratuitous evil cannot exist with God in control. For Nietzsche this supplied a paltry meaning, but at least humanity could will. Thus civilizations emerged with the assistance of the ascetic ideal, a cursory supplier of purpose in suffering. Nietzsche's evolutionary psychology explains for some today why ascetic religions emerged and how they functioned.

CHAPTER 6

The Hourglass of Eternal Recurrence

What is the meaning of history? Few of us get around to pondering the meaning of the entire scope of history, much less our role in its grand schemata. The overwhelming task spins out of control since history reaches as wide as an ocean. Yet in some way we all have a view of "what it *all* means." Many of us commit to stock off-the-shelf worldviews, and they usually provide a prepackaged view of history so we don't have to think about it. Some philosophies, like Marxism, pivot on history seeing it as a class struggle. Varieties of Christianity contain different historical views, such as eschatology. Eschatology studies the end of history to come. While it focuses on the future, it contains a complete view of the arc of history in the past as well. Even secularists view history as evolution and human progress toward some ideal. Nietzsche too looks to a new horizon where the human becomes superhuman. He envisions a new era when people embrace their lives as that which they would wish to eternally recur.

As we encounter Nietzsche's vision of history, understand that the philosophy of history can mean two areas of study. First, it can mean historiography and the study of how to explore past human events. Second, it can mean a vision of the entire scope and significance of the past. We will focus here on this second meaning, though Nietzsche does say significant things about the first. In the next chapter, we will explore Nietzsche's thoughts on politics and human civilization.

Nietzsche creates an eerie transcendence where the scope of all history and personal life eternally recur. Recurrence replaces the Christian eternal life he abandons. His perplexing central doctrine teaches that all of history, especially each person's life, recurs over and over for eternity. Zarathustra heralds this message most remarkably. Recounting the inception of this idea, Nietzsche said that "the thought of eternal recurrence, this highest attainable formula of affirmation . . . was dashed off on a piece of paper with the caption '6000 feet beyond man and time.'"[1] Eternal recurrence emphasizes life here and now, not an afterlife. He gazes down on everything from a perspective of cosmic timelessness, above all, in all, beyond all.

Nietzsche's vision will inspire other thinkers who will explore the question of the meaning of history. In his landmark analysis of the macro patterns of the history of civilization, *Decline of the West*, Oswald Spengler attributes much of his thought to Nietzsche and Goethe.[2] Spengler created vast and complete interpretations of history inspired by Nietzsche's cyclical views of history. Spengler taught that civilizations pass through identifiable cycles of birth, adolescence, maturity, and death. The cyclical nature of history dominates throughout.

How we view history speaks volumes about how we understand the present and the future. While Nietzsche's eternal recurrence portrays history as an endless cycle, unlike Christian linear history, his doctrine applies directly to individuals instead of states, nations, empires, and global history. We will first explore Nietzsche's beliefs about history and move them into his politics. Since political viewpoints usually tie in to history, this ordering is natural.

Friedrich Nietzsche @TwilightOfIdols

Moment, a long, eternal lane leads *backward*: . . . Must not whatever *can* happen have happened, have been done, have passed by before?[3]

↩   ⇄   ♥   •••

We've all experienced *déjà vu*, an ephemeral feeling that we have been somewhere or done something before, while our rational mind tells us we have not. Nietzsche held that every moment leads back to eternity, an endless succession of moments. In that unbroken chain of events, every sequence of events has already happened before. Envision time moving eternally in repeating patterns like a mesmerizing fractal image. All that occurs will recur, *ad infinitum*. In the history of ideas, two basic models of time appear in philosophies of history: the cyclical and the linear.

The cyclical view holds that time occurs in some cycle. This seems natural since the celestial bodies move in cycles. From ancient times people recognized cycles and recurring patterns in life and the world. More than seasons and celestial events, life itself followed a cycle of birth, reproduction, decay, and death. The other model of time follows a linear trajectory. Here time runs in a line, not in circles. The celestial bodies may move in cycles, but time itself occurs linearly. The so-called "arrow of time" flies in a line. Some people attached purpose, or teleology, to the trajectory. Time begins, moves in a direction, and then will end. We often hear this model assumed in statements about the end of time or history. These models of history form deep assumptions in our worldviews, and their undercurrents ebb and flow in our interpretations of events.

Nietzsche viewed his philosophy of history as a nuanced cyclical time that he called an eternal return or eternal recurrence. In the following tweets we will see the implications of his eternal return and how it integrates into other elements of his philosophy.

Friedrich Nietzsche @TwilightOfIdols
For all things have been baptized in the well of eternity and are beyond good and evil.[4]

Eternity engulfs all things, and occasionally they submerge and reemerge, only to repeat endlessly. Events occur and recur with no value. Can eternal time immerse everything beyond good and evil? In

Nietzsche's amoral worldview, what happens must happen out of eternal necessity. The eternal universe submerges all, grinds out, plows under, and repeats all events. There is no good in that, nor evil. It just is. Whatever may arrive, must arrive. *Que será, será*. No meaning or significance arises from this mindless cosmic whirlpool. Teleology (purpose), be gone! It serves no purpose but churns endlessly. The unfathomable, vast cosmic ocean of omnipotent matter, ebbs and flows with time and energy. Life means no more or less than a wandering asteroid. Yes, life wills and rocks don't. Yet as we have seen in other places in Nietzsche's philosophy, even will moves as it must do out of necessity, out of *fati*. In the end, because we differ little from an aimless asteroid drifting in the cosmos, we mean little more. If a roving asteroid collides with the earth tomorrow, annihilating every person alive, nothing significant will take place.

Nietzsche said little about how the unconscious universe could produce consciousness or how a cosmos without a mind could produce rational minds. Nietzsche said precious little about whether our conscious, rational minds produced in an unconscious, irrational universe could be trusted to know anything. At best, we simply happened, and we will recur as all things. We try to imbue things with meaning and purpose, but there really is none from the perspective of eternity. Meaning is a figment of imagination, whether individual or collective. All that is will cease to be, and all that ceases to be, the universe will regurgitate.

Friedrich Nietzsche @TwilightOfIdols
The soul is as mortal as the body. But the knot of causes in which I am entangled recurs and will create me again.[5]

    ↩   ⇄   ♥   •••

We are all a knot of causes, and a big Gordian knot at that. How many contributing causes led to our personal knot of existence? Millions. Trillions! Nietzsche thinks that the cluster of causes is not unique but will occur again. He speaks of a soul but here means it figuratively.

Regardless, if there's any soul, he thinks it perishes like the body. This would mean the soul exists only as a physical thing, perhaps a fleeting brain state.

This view of the soul finds precedent in the ancient school of Epicurean philosophy. The Epicureans believed that all things consisted of atoms and the void. Their prescient grasp of atomism reasoned that all matter must be composed of tiny invisible spheres. These spheres exuded different properties and behaviors due to their sizes and shapes. The name "atom" literally means "uncuttable." Atomists claimed everything, including humans, contained nothing but atoms and void. The soul was another material feature of the body that evaporated upon death. Nietzsche shared a kindred spirit with these ancient materialists, but unlike them, he believed in the eternal return. The filaments of eternal atoms floating in the cosmic void would eventually entwine into the same tangled knot, the same people, eternally.

Friedrich Nietzsche @TwilightOfIdols
I myself belong to the causes of the eternal recurrence.[6]

Zarathustra declares he is swept up the same sequence of causes that brings about the eternal recurrence of all things. In Nietzsche's lifetime, the cause of the cosmos was not understood as it is today. He did not know about the Big Bang, a theory of four decades later. Today, we still do not know exactly what caused the Big Bang, though plausible hypotheses abound on that topic.

The notion that everything in the world will occur again astonishes the imagination. The unfathomable sequence of causes that would have to line up to bring about the exact state of affairs renders this implausible. Given an infinite amount of time in an infinite universe, perhaps it could transpire. This peculiar notion occupies considerable priority in Nietzsche's philosophy, but it may not require literal interpretation.

Nietzsche's eternal recurrence doctrine might function as an existential tool for living. In my life choices and events, maybe I should ask myself whether I would want this to recur. Do I live like I want it to happen endlessly? If I had it to do all over again, would I want my life to be the same? Testing ourselves might help us affirm our choices and ourselves.[7] Sometimes we can choose; other times we cannot; it takes wisdom to know the difference. Once you choose, that particular choice will eternally recur. Perhaps you made that choice infinitely in the past.

Would this decision-making process help? The dreaded unintended consequence always lurks. We do A hoping to get result B, but instead, we get an unintended C. If we choose so that we will never have regrets, we opt for a boring but safe route. Like the herds Nietzsche despises, we play it safe and choose the mundane and banal. Risky choices, by definition, yield a low percentage chance of desirable outcomes. Failure occurs more often, but if you score, you succeed wildly. Nietzsche urges us to live dangerously, to build our houses under Vesuvius. Using the eternal-recurrence question for decision making depends on the level of risk you can tolerate. If Nietzsche intends the eternal-recurrence doctrine to function as an existential tool, a kind of life hack, he urges us to choose in such a way that we could wish our choices to occur over and over for eternity. Choose well.

Friedrich Nietzsche @TwilightOfIdols

I come back eternally to this same, selfsame life, . . . to teach again the eternal recurrence . . . to proclaim the overman again to men.[8]

In classical Greek mythology, which Nietzsche mastered as a professor of philology, Sisyphus resided in *Tartarus*, the dreaded region of Hades. Zeus sent him there for crimes and sins but mostly revenge. There Sisyphus eternally rolled a giant boulder up a steep hill, only to watch it roll back down. He again rolled it up, over and over, unto eternity.

Zarathustra eternally struggles to proclaim the overman to unhearing ears, his Sisyphean task. Each of us must eternally push our own boulder, suffer our own fate, climb our own hill.

Does Nietzsche think eternal recurrence actually happens? Materialistic cosmology in the nineteenth century could allow for such a view. For decades into the late twentieth century, cosmologists speculated about whether the Big Bang would result in a Big Crunch. The oscillating universe theory held that the gravity of all matter in the universe would eventually collapse everything back together in a reverse of the Big Bang. When everything collapsed, the infinite density and force would create another expansion. In this view the universe would ceaselessly expand and contract, or oscillate. Perhaps eternal recurrence could happen in this cosmology. However, this view has been mostly abandoned today due to new data. Exceedingly complex, cosmology requires more scientific instruments to investigate it, such as the Hubble telescope. New telescopes aim to discover new principles about the early universe. Given what we now know about the cosmos, it seems unlikely that it will collapse because it accelerates as it expands. Given scientific cosmology now, recurrence appears impossible. Was Nietzsche just plainly wrong?

As eternal recurrence and the overman intertwine as prime themes in *Thus Spoke Zarathustra*, Nietzsche speaks as if they will actually happen. However, a metaphorical interpretation is plausible too. Nietzsche seems to be asking us to seriously evaluate our life and ask if we would do it all over again. When reflecting on great trials, we often hear people comment, "If I had to do it all over again, I would." If you would not go back and relive your whole life up to this point, then change. Understood this way, the question of eternal return functions as a life hack. It prompts an existential change in life. Regardless, the overman doctrine remains clear. Humanity must evolve. Nietzsche's prescription for the human race's sickness entails an elixir of metamorphosed values. Whether history eternally recurs or not, Nietzsche insists that the new race of overmen must ascend beyond the human race.

Friedrich Nietzsche @TwilightOfIdols
The eternal hourglass of existence is turned upside down again and again, and you with it, speck of dust![9]

I remember from early childhood the opening sequence to the popular and long-running TV series *Days of Our Lives*. I found it on YouTube just to watch the mesmerizing opening. The timeless theme utters, "Like sands through the hourglass, so are the days of our lives." I doubt that the series creators drew the idea from Nietzsche's tweet, but the opening theme evocatively visualizes the idea. Imagine that you exist as a grain of sand in an enormous cosmic hourglass. This hourglass flips over eternally and repeats the trickle of sand endlessly. Your sand grain falls through the opening each time the glass turns, and each time your life recurs. That might explain déjà vu!

Nietzsche bids you to imagine that a spirit or ghost appears to you on a lonely night. Bearing this stark revelation of the eternal return, the spirit utters that you must relive your life eternally, from womb to grave, in endless cycles. Every laugh and every sorrow; every joy and every tear will replay in the same order. Would you see this news as nightmarish? Would that herald haunt you as an ominous curse? Or would that news be a glorious blessing? How would you live differently with that news? Nietzsche's challenge asks us to ponder our life and actions daily and ask ourselves how we should then live. If you have but one moment in your entire life that you would want to relive, then you must accept the whole package. A person may have to suffer ten thousand painful days just to have one day of bliss. Life is a package deal, all or nothing.

We might wonder if Nietzsche's existential diagnostic scenario simply replaces the Christian afterlife or heaven. Nietzsche was raised by his devout Lutheran mother and aunts after the early death of his father. Warmhearted and mildly mystical about their faith, Pietists practiced an introspective Christianity.[10] They asked themselves daily in personal devotions how they should live, knowing they were going to die and go to heaven. With their eyes fixed on eternal life in heaven, this dour world below pales to unimportance. Many Christians live their earthly life as if it means little in the shadow of an eternal life with the Almighty. Living an *ascetic ideal*, they became so heavenly minded that they despise earthly life, their body, and the natural world. To a Christian, the prospect of repeating an earthly life endlessly would be a curse. To a non-Christian like Nietzsche, the same prospect might bring great elation. The eternal return offers a new kind of eternal life that emphasizes earthly life, the body, and its pleasures. Live as if you want to relive this life. Whether or not Nietzsche believed in a literal recurrence, this keynote teaching called people to live as if it were true.

Friedrich Nietzsche @TwilightOfIdols

Joy . . . does not want heirs, or children—joy wants itself, wants eternity, wants recurrence, wants everything eternally the same.[11]

Nietzsche feels that if you joyfully embrace eternal recurrence, then you must value *this* life for exactly what it is, not for what it might lead to. If you value this life in itself, not an afterlife, then you will be authentically joyful. If you want to relive any joyful moment, you must embrace every moment. You will courageously pursue an earthly life fully tilted toward passionate living. When asked if you would do it all over again, you will emphatically proclaim yes, eternally.

CHAPTER 7

Let Freedom Ring
Politics and Government

Worldviews nearly always imply and convey a political element. For Nietzsche, how to politically organize people arises out of his understanding of what human nature is like. His political vision fits with most of the other elements of his worldview. We evolved from inanimate matter to smart animals who possess no ethic or values other than what we create. Our will to power drives us along in a cosmic hourglass. If this is the case, what kind of political organization follows from our nature?

Nietzsche opposes any form of government or society that gives the masses power to control individuals. This includes democracy, socialism, communism, or variations of the three. The herds should not control individuals. Individuals must have freedom to employ their will to power even if it involves exploitation of one individual upon another. Despite the fact that fascists co-opted Nietzsche's ideas for their agenda, he would not have agreed with how they stifled the individual's freedom. In the following tweets, we explore the nuances of his political views.

More tweets on history as it pertains to politics will follow.

Friedrich Nietzsche @TwilightOfIdols
You higher men, learn this from me: in the marketplace nobody believes in higher men . . . The mob blinks: "We are all equal."[1]

↩   ⟲   ♥   •••

For Nietzsche, societies that fiercely embrace and enforce egalitarian values increase equality at the expense of other values. Higher men do not value equality because they rise above the plebian marketplace that clamors for equality. A variety of political schemes envision a society of equal citizens. However, equality itself is ambiguous. Thus, many attempts have emerged to create equality: democracies, socialisms, and communisms. These political systems seek to increase some form of equality to level everyone so they are mostly the same. Nietzsche rails against all attempts to promote equality. In the classic film *The Third Man*, Harry Lime (played by Orson Welles) says,

> Don't be so gloomy. After all it's not that awful. Like the fella says: in Italy for thirty years under the Borgias they had warfare, terror, murder, and bloodshed, but they produced Michelangelo, Leonardo da Vinci, and the Renaissance. In Switzerland they had brotherly love—they had five hundred years of democracy and peace, and what did that produce? . . . The cuckoo clock![2]

Lime vents sentiments akin to Nietzsche: truly great men don't originate in democratic societies that are a little cuckoo. Mediocre people with banal values create a bland and mundane society with little that is noteworthy. Most today don't agree with Nietzsche. He stands with other critics of egalitarian cultures from Plato to Orwell to Ayn Rand, but for his own reasons. Egalitarians aggressively promote equality and disdain what Nietzsche calls the "higher men." These critics believe the superior men will be soon leveled, pulled down by the egalitarian-minded masses that value horizontal relationships, not hierarchical vertical relationships of power. Marx calls this leveling class struggle. Nietzsche's view of history tolerates no role for democracy, socialism, or communism. History should create great individuals, not equal masses.

If people are equal, *what* creates that equality? The answer depends on deep philosophical assumptions. Nietzsche will not answer this question because he thinks people are and should be unequal. Nature itself refuses to equalize people. Inequality naturally occurs, driving a species to survive. Egalitarian societies require countless laws and complex law enforcement to artificially force equality upon people. As he said in the tweet, "The mob blinks: 'we are all equal.'" Only the herd-like mob desires and creates equality.

Friedrich Nietzsche @TwilightOfIdols
The *democratic* movement is the heir to Christianity.[3]
#democracy #slavemorality #sheeple

         •••

The global movement toward democracy overcame major foes in the twentieth century. In two world wars, democracy defeated fascism. Afterward, the long cold war against communism, which involved several proxy wars, ended with victory for democracy. As a new millennium dawned, so did a new challenge for democracy. By some estimates, democracy progresses slowly because of extremist Islam and global terrorism. From Christianity, democracy inherited a mandate to protect everyone equally and to empower the weak. Christianity long taught that all people are *spiritually* equal because they bear the image of God, though defaced or fallen. Each person stands in need of God's grace, regardless of class, race, gender, or education. Slowly, that spiritual equality blossomed into social and political equality in Western civilization. Thus, Nietzsche blames the rise of democracy and egalitarian values on Christianity.

He blames Christianity for incubating modern democracy, seeing it as a blight on the world because it encourages frailty and weakness to flourish. He scorns the "herd morality" and "slave morality," terms fraught with animosity toward traditional morality. Democracy breeds flocks of people who now dominate through laws to protect their weak masses while suppressing the strong. He faults Jewish and Christian morality for breeding the parasitical politics of democracy, socialism, and communism. These political systems mediocritize and debase the human race into a dumb herd of sheeple. However, egalitarianism as a radically equalizing movement leads the world today, even though Nietzsche warns that it leads to destruction.

Friedrich Nietzsche @TwilightOfIdols

"There are no higher men, we are all equal, man is man; before God we are all equal." Before God! But now this god has died.[4]

In this tweet Nietzsche quotes a common voice or opinion of the modern age. He then critiques the notion. In Nietzsche's time people supported democracy and equality with the belief that God made people in his image. Christians also proclaimed that in God's eyes everyone held equal status, for God is no respecter of persons. The apostle Paul wrote, "There is neither Jew nor Gentile, neither slave nor free, nor is there male and female, for you are all one in Christ Jesus."[5] Such passages contributed to the rise of egalitarian ideas in Christian culture. The idea of equality rooted in God finds a central role in America's *Declaration of Independence*. Jefferson pens that equality in the Creator is self-evident. Christian beliefs later inspired abolitionists on both sides of the Atlantic to end slavery.

Nietzsche agrees that the merits of equality rest on God. But God is dead. Without God, egalitarian culture loses its philosophical base. Since Nietzsche didn't think God existed, and that the wretched culture of God was dying fast, equality wouldn't persist. Without an image of God in people, how could equality have a leg to stand on? Moreover, equality, evolution, and natural selection will never harmonize. A species remains hardy and robust through the elimination of the weak, not through equality. Egalitarian social schemes, whether democratic, socialistic, or communistic, only deter humanity from our next evolutionary stage.

We see much emphasis on equality today, yet belief in God declines. Communists since the early twentieth century also sought equality for all within an atheistic framework. Is there a sufficient basis for equality in the secular political arena? It would seem an appeal to God to support equality remains optional now. However, different visions of equality compete and they are each tied to different views of human nature. Nietzsche's evolutionary view of humanity as advanced animals guides him to eschew any natural, social, and political equality.

Friedrich Nietzsche @TwilightOfIdols

A nation is a detour of nature to arrive at six or seven great men. — Yes: and then to get round them.[6]

↩   ⟲   ♥   •••

Nature evolves as human political history, creating great men, and then moves beyond them to even greater things. Nations enable humanity to progress to higher states by creating a short list of great men. However, various philosophies of history try to locate the hinges of history, those turning points where everything changes. For Nietzsche, great individuals lift the human race to new heights. Alexander the Great, Julius Caesar, and Napoleon exemplify the great man who turns everything on his will to power. A great leader advances his people and their cause, leading them to dominate other cultures. However, someday a new leader must overcome the advances of these great leaders.

This "great man" interpretation of history isn't shared by all, but it seems that people still look and long for a great leader who will take them higher and solve their problems. Around election years many hope for a truly great leader. While the common person wants someone with amazing virtues and abilities, Nietzsche reveals that he sees truly great leaders as those who trump traditional virtues, those who go beyond good and evil, and those who will to power.

Napoleon and Alexander the Great willed to power as military conquerors, but other styles of leaders engaged the world differently. In recent times these leaders use a different kind of will to power. Many social reformers will to power employing no force. The peaceful nonviolent protest now uses a soft power. Great men such as Martin Luther King Jr. and Gandhi have turned history on a hinge with a feather touch. Nietzsche would reject their tactics as guilt trips of the weak to overpower the strong.

Friedrich Nietzsche @TwilightOfIdols

Exploitation . . . is a consequence of the intrinsic will to power which is precisely the will of life.[7]

Nietzsche accepts as a primordial fact of all history that cultures dominate and conquer others and that subjugation follows. Humanity slogs through history in a long mêlée of appropriation and suppression of the weaker by the stronger. This conflict plays on every stage of human experience, from personal to global. Neither good nor evil, exploitation is a brute fact.

Cultures die off, just like species. Cultural hegemony usually includes subjugation and control, and sometimes annihilation. Nonviolent domination occurs more frequently. Many smaller cultures around the world today languish on the edge of extinction, steamrolled by enormous mass cultures intentionally or unintentionally swallowing them. The shrinking and death of languages shows this process. The cessation of smaller language groups occurs when global languages drown them. The *UNESCO Atlas of the World's Languages in Danger* catalogs and tracks the shrinking languages of hundreds of ethnic groups.[8] Many wrestle on the edge of extinction. When a language dies, the culture fades. The mass culture that engulfs them unto extinction may not even intend this to happen. The intrinsic thirst for power necessitates it, even if it isn't intentional. To live is to will to power, and it seems the ethic of eat or be eaten prevails.

Friedrich Nietzsche @TwilightOfIdols

The oversaturation of an age with history seems to me to be hostile and dangerous to life.[9]

However we feel about the meaning of history, we live in an age of low historical awareness. We often hear the word *history* spoken as a synonym for "dead and useless," as in, "I hit a tree, and now my car is history." History signifies worthlessness. Perhaps I exaggerate. Don't we have a History Channel on TV after all? This "historitainment" mash-up mixes an often fragmented and predigested entertainment with a sprinkling of history. It does not intend to offer a unified historical consciousness that gives a nation a sense of purpose. Today we agree with Nietzsche and cop an indifferent attitude toward history. However, the Germans in Nietzsche's age took history too seriously. No country nurtured historical consciousness more than Germany.

History resonated deeply in the hearts of many people over the centuries. In Nietzsche's age Germany had produced several grand philosophies of history. Consider one of the most influential, Marxism, where history's role takes center stage. Marx derives much of his philosophical method from the great German philosopher G. F. W. Hegel. Hegel's philosophy of history places German culture at the leading edge of history. Both Hegel and Marx see history as progress, or evolution. For Hegel the progress is spiritual and rational, but for Marx the progress is material, economic, and political. The whole nineteenth-century culture imbibed various intoxicating wines of progress. Even Nietzsche's ideas envision a progression of humanity to a higher animal. Soon two sobering world wars, the Great Depression, fascism, the Holocaust, and the Cold War would decimate this optimism. A long hangover pounded in the head of the twentieth century and lingers now in the twenty-first. Global terrorism continues the thwart progress.

Nietzsche feels that an age that obsesses over history burdens people and chokes the life out of them. History's precedents are hard to escape, and people feel they must carry on traditions and purposes of prior generations. Perhaps people even feel like an appendage, as if they are not great like their forefathers. However, truly great men have one thing in common that we must follow: "To become mature and to flee from that paralyzing upbringing of the present age which sees its advantage in preventing your growth."[10] Nietzsche calls people to throw off the yoke of history and to fashion their own. The abuse of history grips people such that they feel paralyzed to change. If our present age did not get its attitude of breaking with history from Nietzsche, we at least agree with him.

Friedrich Nietzsche @TwilightOfIdols
We moderns have nothing whatever of our own.[11]
#borrowedculture

↩ ↻ ♥ •••

What culture have we produced that is our very own? In the twenty-first century, we consider ourselves as highly advanced, technological, and civilized. Yet the base stock of our culture comes from long ago. We share a few traits with the modern era, though we are not actually modern. Modernity began around 1640 and continued strong up to Kant's death in 1804. It carried through the nineteenth century. Postmodernity began after World War II. This would put Nietzsche at the end of modernity and at the threshold of a postmodern era he helped inspire. The rise of modern science defines the modern age. Can we call science our own?

Nietzsche demurs that modern European culture borrows everything from ancient cultures. Whether art, architecture, literature, drama, philosophy, religion, politics, everything draws from ancient cultural sources. Perhaps modern people improved and modified things, but the seminal germ came from previous ages. Yet in our light-speed culture today, we smugly disregard past times and cultures as somehow inferior. Even the first iPhone is not yet ten years old but seems like an old artifact because of its ubiquity and rapid adoption. How did the modern world recover the knowledge of the deep past to give birth to modernity?

The recapturing of previous cultures developed intentionally as people mined history for scraps of culture. The famed Renaissance project mostly revitalized ancient art forms, whether visual or literary. Classic art forms now give way to more formless styles. Postmodernity subsumes ancient artistic and cultural forms to create new forms of modern art. Old standards of beauty, form, perspective, symmetry, proportion, and style underwent a deconstruction by a crew intent on a bevy of *ad hoc* styles. These bear no distinct characteristics because any new standard violates the core principle of postmodernism that there are no standards. Google postmodern architecture and ponder the images. However, despite the effort to jettison classic forms, postmodernity distorts, mixes, and mocks classic forms—leading us to wonder again with Nietzsche whether we wholly create anything of our own.

Friedrich Nietzsche @TwilightOfIdols

The past speaks . . . as an oracle: only if you are an architect of the future and know the present will you understand it.[12]

↩   ⇄   ♥   •••

Friedrich Nietzsche @TwilightOfIdols

Only he who constructs the future has a right to judge the past.[13] #ListentoOrwell

↩   ⇄   ♥   •••

George Orwell famously warns in his definitive novel *1984* about those who manipulate history for political power. In this genre-defining dystopian novel, Big Brother and the ominous Ingsoc Party manipulate history itself to control people. The intrinsic power and precedent of the past motivates people and manipulates them. The villainous Ingsoc official party line proclaims, "Who controls the past . . . controls the future. Who controls the present, controls the past."[14] Orwell, frightened over the prospect of socialism (Ingsoc meaning English socialism), alerts us to how politicians manipulate us with history. The oft-heard warnings about people who rewrite history or historical revisionists should keep us wary.

While Nietzsche forewarns us of historical manipulation, he urges people to act. He sees that historical interpretations can unnecessarily hinder and exploit people. The meaning of historical precedents is up for grabs. History deeply moves people because it builds identity. If you control people's knowledge of history and manipulate it, you can control them. The implication of the first tweet above is that those who build the future will interpret the past from their position of strength. Oracles always spoke in paradoxes and riddles. Those who dominated would determine the meaning of the oracle's sayings. Thus, whoever came out on top imbued the oracle's words with a convenient meaning. In the second tweet above, Nietzsche reiterates: The one who builds the future will be the one to impose interpretations upon the past, to judge the past. Nietzsche's dictum could well be: "Who owns the present controls the future. Who builds the future controls the past." Nietzsche and Orwell warn us about the manipulation of history for social control.

Friedrich Nietzsche @TwilightOfIdols
Anything that constrains a man to love less than unconditionally has severed the roots of his strength: he will wither away.[15]

Nietzsche exposes a streak of romanticism in his view of history. History isn't about facts but inspiration. In this tweet the "anything" refers to "history." When we overanalyze the past, we suffocate it. Historicizing can mummify life instead of promoting it. Have you ever been interested in some past great person and decided to read their biography, only to have your bubble popped? Your illusion about that person vanished when you learned too much information. When history embalms life, it defeats its purpose. Excessive rational analysis smothers the life out of history, thus rendering it much less inspiring and possibly even depressing. What once inspired and thrilled now disappoints. Rational historicism that brings to light the details, warts and all, brings more harm than good, robbing us of inspiration. Perhaps our culture jettisons history so often for such reasons.

History will never be a science, like chemistry. Attempts to make it so failed. Yet the imposition of methodological naturalism on history generally prevails. Methodological naturalism assumes that naturalism is true in methods of investigation. Scientific assumptions alone can be used in building historical interpretations. Claims of divine intervention in the defeat of a great enemy, or of God doing a miracle, fall outside the pale of reason.

Nietzsche would never accept the return to theistic assumptions that allows miracles in history, but he's against the searing heat of scientific analysis that robs history of its vitality. Do we really want to conclude that the actions of a great man, like Abraham Lincoln, happened purely due to historical circumstances? Many historians accept such conclusions, reducing the world to a machine that churns out all events. Nietzsche says all living things require a mysterious atmosphere around them, and if they are deprived of this misty vapor, they will wither and become unfruitful. History should not consist of fairy tales, but neither should we expel mystique.

Friedrich Nietzsche @TwilightOfIdols

You should love peace as a means to new wars—and the short peace more than the long.[16]

Friedrich Nietzsche @TwilightOfIdols

It is the good war that hallows any cause. War and courage have accomplished more great things than love of neighbor.[17]

Why might Zarathustra advocate war as the basis of a good cause? Is he advocating war at all? Walter Kaufmann, a well-known Nietzsche scholar, rehabilitated Nietzsche from his infamous association with war, including the two World Wars.[18] Kaufmann's humanist Nietzsche promotes no warmongering but compels us to struggle to overcome personal weakness. Thus, Nietzsche's war language metaphorically calls us to struggle to create ourselves.

Other people actively employed Nietzsche's words as a justification for violence. In the early twenty-first century we hate war and prefer to avoid it, though at times military intervention may be necessary and just. Such reticence toward war arose just decades ago, especially during the antiwar 1960s culture. As we might expect, a bellicose interpretation of Nietzsche flips this pacifist moral thinking on its head. The nearly universal human experience of slogging through warring periods exhausted many generations. History enjoyed only a few periods of "short peace," or interregnums.

For Nietzsche, war validates a cause, makes it worthwhile, and amplifies its agenda. War purifies a nation, forces it to be strong, and keeps it focused with a purpose. Many existing nations forged their identity in war. Without those wars there would be no nation. From one perspective the modern nation-state was a machine built for and perfected through war. War purged the weak and allowed the strong to flourish. You either win and flourish . . . or die. It matters little which as long as you live with passion and vigor. Gung ho! However, Nietzsche did not witness the dizzying annihilation of World Wars I and II, where single battles with over a half million casualties became common. Add to this the Holocaust and the aftermath of the wars and the death toll hovers at 100 million people, an incomprehensible decimation of life.

Nietzsche's bellicose statements echoed for decades, their reverberations ripping through the twentieth century with devastating effects. Whether justified or not, Nietzsche has been implicated and blamed for both World War I and II.[19] His popularity in Germany leading up to World War I peaked to levels of cultic mania where he was often compared to Buddha or Christ. German troops treasured and carried his hallmark work, *Thus Spoke Zarathustra*, into the battle trenches, where it rivaled the Bible in popularity. Some 150,000 copies of the deeply inspiring book, printed in a heavy-duty binding, rested each night next to the soldiers' beds along with the Bible and Goethe's *Faust*. Nietzsche's prophetic mystique, aura, and ethic propelled Germans to war with will to power. Later they would self-identify as a super-race of *Übermenshen* who lived dangerously and amorally. The Nazi manipulation of Nietzsche's writings as propaganda hammer-forged a terrible and lasting legacy.

Many intellectuals in Germany, such as Theodor Kappstein, counted Nietzsche as the prime philosopher and motivator of the Nazis and the Great War. His works conflagrated the youth to a "contempt for death . . . to sacrifice on the altar of the whole, towards heroism and quiet, joyful greatness."[20] The assassin Gavrilo Princip, who killed Archduke Franz Ferdinand and his wife Sophie and sparked World War I, admired Nietzsche and deftly recited his erratic *Ecce Homo*.

Should this exploitation of Nietzsche's ideas lay any blame on him, at least in part, for the world wars?[21] Probably not, since that could hardly have been his intention. However, ideas have consequences, and Nietzsche engenders dangerous ideas when he says, "Wars and courage have accomplished more great things than love of the neighbor."[22]

Friedrich Nietzsche @TwilightOfIdols
State is the name of the coldest of all cold monsters. Coldly it tells lies . . . "I, the state, am the people." That is a lie![23]

Friedrich Nietzsche @TwilightOfIdols
But the state tells lies in all the tongues of good and evil; and whatever it says it lies—and whatever it has it has stolen.[24]

What exactly is a legitimate state? The answer says something about a worldview. In Nietzsche, whatever the state is, it is not the *demos*, the people. What exactly is Nietzsche's stance on politics? Though he sends perplexing messages on the matter, he is not a progressive liberal nor leans left politically. Right-wing fascists co-opted some of his ideas and championed him in their cause, though he probably would not have appreciated it. He unfailingly censures liberal ideas of his day that have largely triumphed in the West today. Mark Warren argues that

Nietzsche's politics follow a "neoaristocratic conservatism" that looks to aristocratic social orders in premodern Europe.[25] Nietzsche leans toward conservatism because he eschews the values of liberal democracy, which he sees as a secular form of Christian values like universal rights, social entitlements, and equality.[26] Such herd values diminish humanity, holding us back from advancement to overmen. What a whole society of overmen would resemble finds no analogue in history. That new reality remains unprecedented.

Nietzsche often appears plainly repressive and fascist in his politics, or at least in the political implications of his ideas. We can see why, with his doctrine of will to power, ethical egoism, and master-slave morality. A tension exists between this repressive side of his politics and his stance against state power. He clearly has no love for the state, calling it the "coldest of all monsters." Nietzsche's views of politics fail to be lucid, but he's adamantly against democracy, socialism, and communism.

Friedrich Nietzsche @TwilightOfIdols
State, where all lose themselves, the good and the wicked; state, where the slow suicide of all is called "life."[27]

States contain many parts: bureaucracies, social institutions, militaries, legislatures, laws and law enforcement, courts, judges and judiciaries. The expanding state absorbs a great deal of every citizen's energy, wealth, and time. Perhaps more than these costs, nations can stifle our identity, engulfing us in a collective national character that imbues us with traits, quirks, and dispositions we may not choose. Nietzsche sees the all-engulfing state as destructive to the freedom of the individual. We enter this world, mature, and die in a tight relationship with a state that oversees cradle to grave. Is life robbed or enhanced by this heavy hand? Is citizenship a "slow suicide" that we call life?

In Nietzsche's time more than today, depending on location, states overwhelmed individuals. Naturally, the womb of our culture traps us, but we have more ability to escape now than ever. We can travel with ease. We communicate globally and instantly, though the states listens. A tweet covers the globe in seconds. The globalization of the world, for all of its challenges, opens us up to other cultures more than ever. Still, as Nietzsche says, the state threatens the individual.

Friedrich Nietzsche @TwilightOfIdols
Only where the state ends, there begins the human being.[28] #notafanofgov

Friedrich Nietzsche @TwilightOfIdols
Where the state *ends*—look there, my brothers! Do you not see it, the rainbow and the bridges of the overman.[29]

States appear in many forms and names, yet they are usually a blend of three basic principles of rule. If you think the political options are limited just working with three prime types, remember that innumerable colors can be created with three primary colors. Long ago, political philosophers analyzed the ways to govern people and discovered that there are three basic ways to govern. A state ruled by one person is a monarchy. A state ruled by group of rulers is an aristocracy. Finally, a state run by the entire population is a democracy. These exist in many variations and combinations, and history has experimented to create many hybrid political forms. Each controls people, and the individual can suffer stifling tyranny in all, even a tyranny of the majority.

Nietzsche dislikes states because they stifle individuals, but he still thinks that states played a vital role in human history. In the evolution of beast to human, and human to overman, the state performs a service. The state organized beasts into a human community. We crossed a boundary between beast and human when we organized into states. States bring some security from crime and invasion. Synergy from cooperating citizens yields greater wealth and function. Yet after several millennia of government and the rise of the modern nation state, states reign too powerful to allow the next stage beyond the human. A state creates laws to control people and piles laws upon laws, taxes upon taxes, for centuries, thus choking individuals. Does the state place too many burdens on us, thus snuffing out life and liberty?

While Nietzsche abhors governments, we may wonder if he proposes anarchy. When state control of the individual ceases, the overman can arise—"the rainbow and bridge to the overman begins." Being cautious not to hastily label Nietzsche as an anarchist, other components of his worldview do that support anarchy.

Nietzsche trumpets the victory of the individual over the collective, convincing us to not be pressed into the enslaving mold of the status quo. If we liberate people, consequences will follow. Unchecked freedom inflates inequality, but radical inequality presents no problem for Nietzsche. He exulted in the triumph of the will to power and the ascendency of those who overcome all things to become overmen.

Friedrich Nietzsche @TwilightOfIdols

Liberal institutions stop being liberal as soon as they have been set up: afterwards there is no one more thorough in damaging freedom.[30]

            •••

Imagine a large sector of land that contains a pristine mountain and a valley. Now imagine the mountain being systematically detonated with dynamite. The debris from the mountain is moved to the valley to fill it. One vast plain now exists—no mountain, no valley—just level ground. Liberal institutions level society like this in the name of progress and morality, and Nietzsche abhors it. What institutions do this? Education, healthcare, taxes, and countless government bureaucracies overseeing all areas of life operate on this principle. If you look for it, you find that equality reigns as an unquestioned value in liberal democratic societies. If you do not notice, it may be because equality is a shared assumption—a value so deeply assumed that nobody talks about it.

Nietzsche unveils the irony. Before liberal institutions establish themselves in society, they appear to fight *for* freedom, but once they take root, they *take away* freedom and undermine the will to power. They destroy freedom by enforcing equality and a "contemptible kind of well-being that only shopkeepers, Christians, cows, women, Englishmen, and democrats dream about."[31] For Nietzsche, liberalism, secular or Christian, fosters herd-animalization and creates public policy, bureaucracies, and a cultural milieu of stifling institutions.

Concerning equality, he declares "no more venomous poison in existence" threatens humanity because equality *appears* to most people to be justice itself.[32] Justice appears to grow in proportion to equality, but it actually diminishes. Freedom threatens to decrease equality because people who have freedom to direct their lives will engage in choices that lead to highly unequal consequences. Thus, freedom enables a certain kind of inequality. Choices in life accumulate into natural inequalities. Equality increases at the cost of less freedom. An inverse proportional relationship ensues between these fundamental values. Nietzsche eschews a state that removes freedom to create a herd of equal people.

Friedrich Nietzsche @TwilightOfIdols
Human society is a trial . . . and what it tries to find is a commander. A trial, O my brothers, and *not* a "contract."[33]

Social-contract theory has evolved since the Enlightenment. The Enlightenment refers to a movement within the modern era that includes the rise of science and the rational organization of all human concerns, including politics. It cultivated deep confidence in progress. Society can progress through rational organization, collaboration, and cooperation for the common good. All of this general goodwill and agreement must be spelled out in a social contract, somewhat akin to a constitution and the laws generated under its umbrella. Nietzsche, standing at the end of the modern era, rejects society as a contract.

Social-contract theory struck a chord in the Enlightenment, stating that legitimate government should be by consent, or by a contractual agreement of those who are ruled. The largest social contract might well be the United Nations, a kind of global social contract. Each nation writes its own contract, perhaps a constitution or charter. The UN as a conglomerate of nations would create the highest tier of contract, with members being not individuals but nations. Kant called for a global republic made up of individual member republics. His treatise *Perpetual Peace* envisioned an international body that would create laws to govern the member republics. Only after World War I did world leaders attempt such an idea with the League of Nations. It ultimately failed, but a new attempt emerged after World War II with the United Nations.

Nietzsche spurns social-contract reasoning despite its growing popularity during his time. He disagrees with social contracts and their usual form as democracies. Such governments thwart true progress. He thinks what societies really need is an outstanding leader. Remember that Nietzsche said a nation is a detour of nature to arrive at six or seven great men and then get around them. Even democracies, which are supposed to be ruled by the people, elect presidents with immense executive power. Presidential elections receive the greatest attention because people really need a commander, not a contract. Nietzsche's political views here parallel his views on ethics and human nature. People should be left to natural processes, including natural power and rule. In nature the strong flourish and the weak perish. The former exploit the latter. The strong deserve to rule. The strong have no interest in entering into social contracts with the weak who will be better off with a powerful leader than with a social contract.

CHAPTER 8

Nietzschean Insights on Life

Nietzsche reflected on many topics and issues in life. He leaves few stones unturned, writing prolifically on life's many twists and turns. These tweets don't quite fit in the previous chapters, but they offer a range of noteworthy insights. I will comment on some and let others stand alone.

Friedrich Nietzsche @TwilightOfIdols

The secret of the greatest . . . enjoyment of existence is: *to live dangerously!* Build your cities under Vesuvius![1] #livedangerously

---

Ships remain safe in harbors . . . but that is not what ships are built for. Get out there! Launch your ships into uncharted waters, to where the map says, "Here be Dragons!" Nietzsche perpetually appeals to those who laugh at death, the big risk takers, those who go to extremes, the young, and those who #livedangerously.

Nietzsche, existentialist prophet extraordinaire, urges us to press the seal of our resolute will onto the wax of the world rather than passively allowing ourselves to be molded to the world. Either you mold the world or it will mold you. Existentialism asserts our sheer will to triumph over nature, ourselves, and the will of others. Tenacity of will overcomes the forces of nature only with great suffering, but our progress requires struggle.

We launch our rockets to the Moon, to Mars, to infinity. As John F. Kennedy proclaimed, "We choose to go to the Moon . . . not because [it is] easy, but because [it is] hard."[2] At least the lunar astronauts came home. New projects to colonize Mars, such as Mars One, require astronaut candidates to never return. One-way ticket. Live dangerously indeed. Nietzsche's aggressive tilt toward risk hopes to overcome anything that would control us. Risk might pay off enormously—or crash and burn abysmally.

The entire human experience wrestles with the choice between living a comfortable, secure life of mediocrity versus burning out in a blaze of glory. Even ancient stories reflect this existential dilemma. The classical warrior and hero of Homer's *Illiad*, Achilles received a rare opportunity: an unfated choice between glory leading to his early death or a comfortable life in old age and abject obscurity.[3] He lost faith in the whole pursuit of military honor and glory won in battle. The commander Agamemnon had stripped Achilles of his greatest prize, Briseis, a beautiful girl who symbolized his military honor. The whole system of honor, merit, and glory collapsed as a farce. Achilles quit.

The relentless predicament of existence and survival cuts across every age as an element of the human condition. Eventually Achilles chose glory, yet at an unbearable cost. He reentered battle to recover the slain body of his best friend, Patroclus. The abject emptiness of death in war swallowed his life. True to the prophecy, if Achilles chose glory at the cost of an early death, his fame would live forever. That I'm telling his story 3,200 years later should indicate he chose glory. Soon after, Paris shot an arrow into Achilles's heel, his only vulnerable spot, and he died. "It's better to burn out than fade away" echoes Neil Young's *Rust Never Sleeps* album.[4] Our universal human condition presses most of us into choosing safety, into what Nietzsche condemns as a herd life. We huddle in security and breed false values for a safe harbor. For Nietzsche, the greatest live dangerously.

 Friedrich Nietzsche @TwilightOfIdols
Cynicism is the only form in which common souls come close to honesty.[5]

            •••

Friedrich Nietzsche @TwilightOfIdols
Not by wrath does one kill, but by laughter.[6]

Laughter and derision devastate people more than wrathful confrontation. To ridicule someone creates a situation of greater vulnerability than violent attack. Ridicule attacks someone from the inside instead of the outer attack of violence.

Many critics through history have manipulated crowds with satire and humor to devastate opponents. Aristophanes in ancient Greece undermined Socrates in his satirical play "Clouds." Erasmus attacked the popes and the abusive elements of the Roman Catholic Church in his *In Praise of Folly*. The inimical and derisive wit of Voltaire sliced and diced many opponents. In his *Candide*, he rips Leibniz's *Theodicy* for saying that this is the "best of all possible worlds."

As the power of satire became clear, many social critics adopted it. Hugely successful, *The Daily Show* with Jon Stewart deftly exploited the technique to excoriate politicians and cultural elites while hiding behind the defense of "it is just humor." Caricatures look ridiculous and evoke laughter, instantaneously invalidating and eviscerating the target.

Why does humor kill more effectively than wrath? Nietzsche grasps the fact that wrath will be met by an opposing wrath. Angry opponents fuel each other and escalate violence. Satire and ridicule, however, have a different dynamic. Bringing derisive laughter against an opponent can do two things. If he or she gets angry and lashes out, it causes more laughter. The other effect simply unplugs and deflates an opponent. Laughter withers, since it is hard for a rational person to stay rational in any rejoinder.

Savvy targets of ridicule roll with the punches and laugh with the satirist. People don't laugh long at people who laugh at themselves. Of course, this isn't easy when it isn't fair, but it softens the blow while showing any audience that you have thick skin. It may stop the next attack since the ruse didn't work.

Friedrich Nietzsche @TwilightOfIdols
Not a few who wanted to drive out their devil have themselves entered into swine.[7]

Zarathustra proclaims that we diminish ourselves to lesser beings when we get rid of our devilish nature. We cast out our demons, and then we enter into swine. This tweet alludes to a biblical passage, Luke 8:27–33, in which Jesus cast a group of demons out of a man and sent the demons into a herd of pigs. The pigs then rushed down a hill and ran into the sea and drowned. Zarathustra pursues a wandering mystic life, like Jesus, but teaches the opposite principles. In Nietzsche's relentless attack on Christianity, he quips that we would be better off living with demonic natures than to cast them out and become like pigs ourselves.

Friedrich Nietzsche @TwilightOfIdols
When you gaze long into an abyss the abyss also gazes into you.[8]

On episode 200 of the CBS series *Criminal Minds* the character J.J. quotes this tweet after narrowly escaping kidnappers.[9] First responders, police, ER staff, soldiers, and care providers of all types under the highest stress take a front-row seat to the dark drama of human misery. Many daily confront the abysses of human experience. When life events seem randomly absurd, when calamities threaten us, we feel like an empty abyss, and the absurdity of human existence echoes down the long, hollow corridors of the aching heart. Nietzsche must have felt this way many times in his desolate years. Such experiences drive some to existential despair. Some people give in to despair, abandoning hope of any significance to life, even embracing darkness.

Other resonances of Nietzsche's abyss occur in various dramatic productions. The *Star Wars* character, Yoda, warns that if you peer into the dark side, the dark side looks back. The Jedi Anakin Skywalker gazed too long and morphed into Darth Vader. The principle also appears dramatically in the movie series *The Lord of the Rings*. When Frodo employs the power in the One Ring, the Eye of Sauron stares back into Frodo's soul to draw him. Another example, the successful TV series *Breaking Bad* tells the story of Walter White, a chemistry teacher who suffers from cancer. In the despair of terminal illness, he becomes a maker of illegal methamphetamine to finance his family. The character grows darker and morphs into a villain. The recurring theme clearly speaks: embrace darkness and darkness will ensnare you in a vicious circle.

Nietzsche gazed long into an abyssal void of meaning, beyond good and evil. Peering into the abyss of human despair, as existential philosophers often do, brings the risk of slipping into it. We psychologically attach to whatever we dwell on. We can lustfully embrace what destroys us. Nihilism is not where Nietzsche wants to end. We see that he tries to vault over the chasm. How can we turn our gaze from the dark abyss to the sun? For Nietzsche and the existentialists he inspires, the path out of the shades of despair arises from sheer will. Will to power. Will to life. One ascends out of the abyss by will. There's no meaning down there. No life. Just do it: climb out, and by pluck of will invent meaning.

Friedrich Nietzsche @TwilightOfIdols

In truth, there was only *one* Christian, and he died on the cross.[10]

For Nietzsche, only one person authentically lived the life that Christ proclaimed: Christ himself. Nietzsche attacks Christianity far more than he attacks Jesus; in *The Antichrist*, he assaults it from every angle. It would be appropriate to think of the book title as *Antichristianity*. Only the authentic life Jesus lived and his death on the cross should be called Christian, not some set of doctrines or beliefs. Nietzsche here foreshadows a prevailing sentiment of our time. True Christianity lives not in orthodoxy (correct teaching) but in orthopraxy (correct actions). Authentic Christians live, act, and practice life like Jesus in such a way that falsifies faith in a set of dogmatic beliefs. Nietzsche's vitriol falls on the abuse of the institution more so than Christ himself, for he does not think we can really know much about the historical Jesus. Nietzsche did not believe Christ was the Son of God or that he was resurrected; rather he was Jesus, a historical figure who didn't do miracles or prophesy about the future.

To reduce Christ from Son of God and Savior to a mere man who tried to reform his society was nothing new in Nietzsche's day. German universities where Nietzsche studied buzzed with theological activity from those who undermined orthodox Christian claims. One of the most influential was F. C. Baur, who led the famous Tübingen school of New Testament interpretation. Baur's main thesis was that Peter's Jewish conception of Christianity clashed with Paul's Gentile conception. These two competing visions coalesced and canceled each other into a blended synthesis in the late first century. In 1835, David Strauss, a student of Baur's, wrote *Life of Jesus* in an attempt to uncover the "historical Jesus." As a young scholar around twenty, Nietzsche studied theology and aided Strauss's opponents by writing against him. Thus we see that Nietzsche absorbed ample exposure to critical scholarship and demythologization in theology.

Nietzsche's grievances in his notoriously entitled book, *The Antichrist*, fall mostly on the Christian church, the institution that employed Christ as an ethical, religious, and political system that demeans and weakens humanity. Of course, Nietzsche employs hyperbole and metaphor, which can be easily misconstrued. Thus, he's not a Christian and does not believe in Christ as Savior, but his gripe is against a civilization that has killed God and internalized Christian ideals that don't even reflect Jesus.

Friedrich Nietzsche @TwilightOfIdols
We are from the start illogical and therefore unfair beings . . . It is one of the greatest and most insoluble disharmonies of existence.[11]

By any measure fairness is hard to come by. Humans do not naturally think in logical patterns. We can, but it requires rigorous education and training. It's like doing math on guitar strings. Even with great intellects, we lapse into nonrational patterns that cloud our thinking. When we attempt to apply and execute justice for others, we operate under so many misperceptions that we can rarely be just. We usually operate with a few bare facts, not even all of them. Many valuable facts escape our grasp, and we warp justice with our subjective states of mind, moods, and hidden motives. Embedded motives in our consciousness skew judgment and create prejudices. Even with all the knowable facts and a stable state of mind, we may still reason to illogical conclusions.

We encounter many kinds of injustice because societies must administer justice in various ways: merit, criminal justice, social justice, and tort justice. We all want a just society. We want to be treated fairly, even though that concept is unclear to most. We've all heard the cliché that life isn't fair and to get over it. But do we ever really? Justice constantly eludes us due to the frailties of the human condition. Yet we must pursue it. Nietzsche here tells us to abandon the idea of justice. There isn't any justice because there isn't any morality. His vaunted will to power encourages things most would deem unjust. We fail at justice because we fundamentally lack the rational capacities to achieve it. We are primordially illogical.

Friedrich Nietzsche @TwilightOfIdols
The most serious parody I ever heard was this: "In the beginning was the nonsense, and the nonsense was with God, and the nonsense was God."[12]

↩   ⇄   ♥   •••

Friedrich Nietzsche @TwilightOfIdols
All great things bring about their own demise . . . That is the law of life, the law of necessary self-overcoming.[13]

↩   ⇄   ♥   •••

Nietzsche says Christian morality will implode because it spawns it's opposite in nihilism. A stripe of Hegelianism runs through him. Here we see Hegel's dialectic process where great things cause their opposite to arise. Once engendered, the two conflict until they both cancel out and preserve each other in a new idea. Nietzsche argues that Christian morality leads to a dead end. The overcoming of this morality will spawn two centuries of transvaluation.

Friedrich Nietzsche @TwilightOfIdols
There are more idols than realities in the world . . . [to] *hammer,* and, perhaps, to hear as a reply that famous hollow sound.[14]

I take Nietzsche's Twitter handle from his last personally published work, *Twilight of the Idols* or *How to Philosophize with a Hammer.* He published this just before his mental breakdown in 1889. The last phrase of this title, "how to philosophize with a hammer," has taken on its own meaning over the years. Given Nietzsche's penchant for hyperbole, it would be easy to see this phrase as a bombastic claim that he would smash idols as with a giant sledgehammer. However, his iconoclastic project hammer taps idols as with a tuning fork to see if they ring hollow. He listens as with a stethoscope to the idol's interior. If hollow, he smashes it. What are these idols? Idols are the ideas, doctrines, and traditions that cultures have embraced so long that they assume their truth even though they are lies. Nietzsche explains, "*Twilight of the Idols*—in plain words: the old truth is coming to an end."[15] He promotes the transvaluation or relocation of value creation in individuals instead of the idols of traditional morality or any moral system.

Before Nietzsche, other iconoclastic thinkers tried to smash different idols that hinder human progress. In Francis Bacon's monumental contribution to modern science, *Novum Organum* (1620), he identified and denounced four types of idols that thwart human progress: idols of the tribe, the cave, the marketplace, and the theater. In Bacon, each of these deceives or misleads us away from scientific progress. Whether Nietzsche follows

Bacon in identifying further cultural idols for destruction may be speculated, though there are parallels in their projects. Claiming to be the first to hold the touchstone of truth, Nietzsche taps around with his hammer to find misleading psychological figments of society's collective imagination. He finds hollow idols in moral systems, cultural figures, values, and mores.

 Friedrich Nietzsche @TwilightOfIdols
To sin against the earth is now the most dreadful thing.[16]
#ecology #animalrights #climatechange

         •••

Zarathustra urges his followers to consider the earth and be faithful to it. His earthbound worldview values this world, not an otherworld. We live at an all-time high of eco-consciousness. As it grows, we become deeply aware of how fragile our ecosystem is and how dependent we are. Eco-nihilism looms. The warnings come almost daily. As the threat of climate change menaces with its endless implications, we enact environmental laws and policies on local and global levels. I ardently recycle and find ways to conserve natural resources. We protect animals and often afford them better treatment, higher status, and more rights than some humans. Consumer products find their way into our hearts and homes by being eco-friendly and green. Green marketing dominates the mainstream, and at its worst descends into greenwashing. We cringe and grow outraged over ecological disasters and crisis. To sin against the environment is now among the worst crimes. Nietzsche foreshadows this spirit because he sees that without God, sin can only be against the environment as that which mothers us.

The ecological movement spawned an array of submovements. Its roots reach down several generations into the early 1960s, though some would trace it all the way to Thoreau's *Walden* of 1854. Rachel Carson's 1962 book, *Silent Spring,* alerted people of the deadly effects of DDT.[17] Eventually the book spawned the ecological movement in America. Nietzsche foresees the gravity of sinning against the earth, though it was not one of his main themes. Though denying belief in sin *per se*, his common sense says that damage to the earth is the "most dreadful." In his materialistic worldview we evolved from the earth and depend on it every second for life. Damaging it chokes the very soil, air, and water that nourish our growth.

Friedrich Nietzsche @TwilightOfIdols
One thing is needful. "Giving style" to one's character—a great and rare art![18]

Creation of the self with an artistic flair inspires Nietzsche to existential heights. We should make something of ourselves, something that satisfies us individually as we consciously craft our personage into our own vision of whom we want to be. Of course, this requires will and fortitude. Through long habituation we can forge qualities into our character. Whether we choose sports, education, talents, fitness, or other ways to craft ourselves, we give style to our character. Western culture has long held to individualism, but Nietzsche's art of self-creation carries it further than just adding on some extra abilities throughout life. His greatest artistic creation is himself. The existentialist tones here grow rich and saturate with deep color.

Friedrich Nietzsche @TwilightOfIdols
One loves ultimately one's desires, not the thing desired.[19]

What good is delicious food to us if we are not hungry? The objects of desire appeal to us in proportion to the strength of our desire itself. Imagine a boy who's been given money to buy any candy he wants. Because he's sick, however, the thought of eating candy nauseates him.

Philosophers throughout history have explored the strange relationship between our desires and the things desired. Pleasure is a strange experience upon closer analysis because of its dependence on desire. Perhaps more bizarre is the intensifying of pleasures through pain. Suppose you have been invited to a holiday feast of epic proportions, with every kind of yummy food you can imagine. The feast starts at 7:00 p.m. tomorrow. What will you do before the feast? Some of us will fast. When we arrive at the feast completely famished, we binge. We enjoy the swing from intense hunger to intense pleasure. Why do we do this? We desire the desire itself and manipulate the desire itself for maximal effect. Some people escalate the intensity and addict themselves to whatever desire they pursue.

This pleasure-and-desire relationship led many philosophers to abandon desire and pleasure as a path to happiness. Nietzsche abandons no desires, but promotes them.

Friedrich Nietzsche @TwilightOfIdols
Man thinks the world itself is overwhelmed with beauty—he *forgets* he is its cause.[20]

         •••

For Nietzsche we cause all beauty by willing it to be so; when we treasure and worship something, we beautify it. Just as humans alone give meaning to things, we alone impart beauty to them. More than simply valuing beautiful things, people, and places, we impart immeasurable worth upon what we deem beautiful. For there really is no beauty independent of things. Nietzsche's position agrees with the nominalist argument over the universals and particulars. Nietzsche thinks no universals exist. There is no essence to anything, including beauty. What people call beautiful is merely what is beneficial to an individual in some way.

Nietzsche does not echo old clichés like "Beauty is in the eye of the beholder," but rather thinks beauty is in the *will* of the beholder. He pushes the insight farther than individual subjective perception. The entire human race bestows an all-too-human spin on the world. Other creatures perceive a different kind of beauty or none at all. People might enjoy flowers as beautiful, but to a frog they are not. Beauty is a figment of our imagination and an act of our will. As Nietzsche says, "Nothing is beautiful, only man is beautiful: all aesthetics rests on this naivety; . . . Nothing is ugly except degenerating man—thus the realm of aesthetic judgment is delimited."[21]

You might be tempted to discount Nietzsche's perspective on beauty, but consider his influence on artists of all types including literature, music, dance, visual arts, theater, and cinema. His immense influence contributed to the rise of contemporary and abstract art where many look to him for inspiration.

Friedrich Nietzsche @TwilightOfIdols
"This is *my* way; where is yours?"—thus I answered those who asked me "the way." For *the* way—that does not exist.[22]

Nietzsche says subjectivity is the only way. There is no objective way per se, only one's personal way. If I center my values and my truth on my needs and my will, they can't be universalized. They can't be applied to even one other person. This sentiment comes down to us today through postmodern culture where individual subjective perspectives trump ideas of objective truth. We may hear people remark, "That is true for you, but not for me. I don't personally think _____ is okay, but I'm not going to impose my view on others." This pervasive attitude informs many today on social and moral issues. This transvaluation allows people to retreat into an unassailable castle of personal opinion.

Friedrich Nietzsche @TwilightOfIdols
We should call every truth false which was not accompanied by at least one laugh.[23]

The very idea of Nietzsche, nihilism, and existentialism, smacks of foreboding depression. Yet a fair amount of his writing encourages people to be joyful.

Friedrich Nietzsche @TwilightOfIdols
I love the valiant; but it is not enough to wield a broadsword, one must also know against whom.[24]

Shakespeare said, "Discretion is the better part of valor." Nietzsche agrees that knowing when and where to pick your battles saves you for more worthy battles. An oft heard piece of wisdom when confronting opponents says, "This is not a hill on which to die." Choose your battles wisely.

Friedrich Nietzsche @TwilightOfIdols
That everyone may learn to read . . . corrupts not only writing but also thinking.[25]

Nietzsche perhaps presciently remarked that with another century of readers the spirit would stink. In one century since Nietzsche, we have gone from being book readers to image viewers. Reading indeed changed the world. With the introduction of the printing press, more people became readers as book ownership increased. While this created a more educated population, some unintended consequences followed that concerned Nietzsche. The decline to base forms of writing to reach larger audiences accelerated. Think of examples like romance novels. As new mediums of communication arose, so baseness increases. What would Nietzsche say about radio, film, TV, and the Internet?

Some five hundred years after Gutenberg we watch images rather than read words. We are more feelers than thinkers. Printing presses hum down to a halt now in this age of imagery. As Neil Postman explains in his classic media and culture study, *Amusing Ourselves to Death*, we have moved from a text-based to an image-based society.[26] In an image-based culture, people no longer think logically but merely feel. Images fuel emotions. Moving from a reading culture to a watching culture shifts attitudes and brain matter. After these five centuries since Gutenberg, illiteracy rates remain a threat and our ability to write has declined. Has our ability to think declined? Are we amusing ourselves to death?

Friedrich Nietzsche @TwilightOfIdols
Our faith in others betrays in what respect we would like to have faith in ourselves.[27]

The way we trust others shows how we trust ourselves. Ever an acute observer of human nature, Nietzsche here sees our reflexive inner tendencies. If I don't trust myself, how can I trust others?

Friedrich Nietzsche @TwilightOfIdols
I know my destiny . . . something formidable . . . I am no man, I am dynamite.[28]

Nietzsche viewed himself as a destiny for the earth. His autobiographical work, *Ecce Homo*, expresses many grandiose statements about his life, work, impact, destiny, and fame. As the last book he wrote, *Ecce Homo* would not be published until 1908, twenty years after he wrote it and eight years after he died. Many of his statements appear megalomaniacal to us today, such as this tweet. Remember that he did not live in a democratic age or culture that looks sourly upon those who unabashedly self-promote. His keen awareness that his ideas would powerfully influence the world proved true. He saw his work as a kind of dynamite, something that moves mountains with destructive force in order to build.

Nietzsche's dynamite disintegrates old values to make way for a new value. This transvaluation, or reevaluation, topples and destroys all former traditions as a hammer, smashing idols, clearing the way for egoism and will to power. That Western societies have followed this project since his death should be easy to see in the march of individual freedoms in various forms such as feminism, civil rights, reproductive rights, free sex, sexual orientation, and gender, to name a few. Each of these promotes individuals by giving them the ability to revise or reject traditional values. Nietzsche's project of transformative egoistic individualism triumphed and has become the new normal.

Friedrich Nietzsche @TwilightOfIdols
Of all that is written I love only what a man has written with his blood. Write with blood, and you will experience that blood is spirit.[29]

Friedrich Nietzsche @TwilightOfIdols
Madness is something rare in individuals—but in groups, parties, peoples, ages it is the rule.[30] #Ageofmadness

CHAPTER 9

A Deeper Dive into Nietzsche's Protean Worldview

The tweets from the chapters above show the sketch lines of Nietzsche's worldview. He weaves a tapestry from the threads of the overman, will to power, eternal return, *amor fati*, perspectivism, the transvaluation of values, and other ideas. If time allowed, other intriguing topics abound, such as his philosophy of mind, music, Greek culture, and aesthetics. We'll turn now to another perspective and straightforwardly explore his worldview implications in light of current culture. I don't pretend that mine is the only plausible response or that I can exhaustively evaluate him. No evaluation achieves total immunity to some of the dynamics Nietzsche identified. We'll proceed with the awareness of these challenges. He defies being pinned down; his provisional and perspectival outlook has inspired a vast body of interpretation over the last 120 years. Opening the door of Nietzsche's works, you enter a mansion of mirrors where his Protean tendencies create a giant and unwieldy flow of images. I've stumbled through this maze, and I have found a way through. Anyone who ventures into that mansion will certainly wander another path, for Nietzsche constructs mazes rather than labyrinths.

Revisiting themes above, I endeavor to interact with his worldview in an appropriate way. Can we fairly evaluate Nietzsche's vision of the world when he is speculative, experimental, malleable, and intentionally nonsystematic? Despite these hurdles, Nietzsche himself employed a worldview understanding. Naugle writes, "Nietzsche believes worldviews are cultural entities which people in a given geographical location and historical context are dependent upon, subordinate to, and products of."[1] Nietzsche views life in a perspectival way, eschewing systems like those of Kant or Hegel because they force conformity when anomalies arise, like some Procrustean bed. He equalizes systems, religions, cultures, and other worldviews. Perspectivism sees every attempt to gain knowledge as trapped in a bubble of personal or cultural perspective. Systems hinder intellectual honesty, and Nietzsche refuses to sell out or buy in to one. When we will to truth and "accept a faith just because it is customary, [it] means to be dishonest, to be cowardly, to be lazy."[2] He refuses will to truth and chooses will to power, his highest virtue. If someone commits to a system of round holes, you can bet he will round off the corners of square pegs that won't fit. Nietzsche leaves pegs square. A hammer sees every problem as a nail. His hammer strikes much more than nails. He highly values and practices intellectual honesty, and if that leads to contradictions, so be it. He believes that a great man's errors far outweigh a small man's truths. However, despite his system smashing, he expresses patterns that inevitably gel into persistent and consistent messages. As one who promoted worldview thinking, he can't *not* have a worldview. His perspectivism adopts some perspective.

Evaluating Nietzsche's Worldview

Even Nietzsche adopts criteria for evaluating other worldviews. Nietzsche might deem my evaluation unacceptable. For example, if he believes that no moral order exists, is it proper to analyze his morality? If he believes that only physical things exist, can we speak of his quest for transcendence in the eternal return? If he thinks knowledge springs from values, can we critique his epistemology? Any evaluation risks difficulties, yet abandoning evaluation altogether risks greater problems. Nietzsche prefers his philosophy not to be put into old boxes that he tries to destroy. New wine should not go into old wine skins. He's hard to pin down. Yet he expounds weighty views on metaphysics, epistemology, and morality. For all his attacks on values, he values *something* as normatively good;

namely, will to power, godlessness, *amor fati*, the overman, amorality, transvaluation, and the eternal return. Whatever opposes these is bad.

Friedrich Nietzsche @TwilightOfIdols
What, then, is truth? A mobile army of metaphors . . . a sum of human relations . . . illusions about which one has forgotten.[3]

↩   ⇄   ♥   •••

To fairly evaluate Nietzsche we will examine the *unity* of his worldview. Why unity? Because he implicitly values unity, and a worldview deserves to be evaluated consistently with its values. Without unity any worldview falls apart. Unity surpasses disunity and integration exceeds disintegration. Greater unity indicates a more viable, practical, and desirable worldview. We'll see why unity operates as a reasonable measure below. Nietzsche's worldview needs unity to avoid disintegration, and we will examine his worldview for three kinds of unity: coherence, correspondence, and practicality. Coherence simply means that something or someone is free of contradictions. Correspondence entails an agreement between what someone says and what we see in the world. Practicality weighs the plain ability of a worldview to be lived out daily.

Nietzsche may not agree to these three unities, since I characterize them from my own worldview. If cats rate a dog, they grade him poorly because the canine lacks feline values. Birds would esteem cats even lower for lacking flight. Likewise, everyone harbors biases. While we can't fully access Nietzsche's original meaning or intent without slightly projecting our own ideas and culture onto the image, such dangers always lurk, whether reading ancient texts or talking face-to-face.

Friedrich Nietzsche @TwilightOfIdols
No, facts is [sic] precisely what there is not, only interpretations. We cannot establish any fact "in itself."[4]

↩   ⇄   ♥   •••

Our interpretations spring from our desires and values. Despite these prejudices, we strive to neutralize them by being aware of them. Awareness of our assumptions allows us to better understand and evaluate another's. I assume and value these three unities as insightful perspectives into worldviews.

Any devotee of a worldview probably believes that it works, makes sense, and corresponds to reality. Can the unities of coherence and correspondence serve as criteria to evaluate Nietzsche? Is practicality too subjective? If not, then Nietzsche and all worldviews escape analysis. A pluralistic approach sees all worldviews as equally valid or equally invalid. In postmodernist terms, there is no metanarrative (a superior worldview) that can evaluate other narratives (worldviews). Thus, one person's absurdity is another person's coherence. One may believe an incoherent worldview because he or she thinks reality is incoherent. Nietzsche contends we subjectively perceive all from within.

Thus we can drift into an infinite echo chamber of criteria. What are our criteria? What is our criterion for choosing that set? If we deconstruct until all lays leveled, we disintegrate deconstruction itself. This infinite regression refutes itself. Persistent skepticism itself exists as a worldview that tries to impose its valueless value on other worldviews. This follows from interpretations of Nietzsche running through our culture. Therefore, let us approach the question of evaluation from another perspective.

"Enough! Enough!" as Nietzsche often declares. He himself implicitly values these three unifying qualities. He holds others accountable for incoherence, lack of correspondence, and impracticality. He targets theism, the preferred foil for his views, because he does not think its ideas correspond with materialistic reality. He confronts traditional morality as a map of human behavior that never corresponds with humanity. Nietzsche chides Schopenhauer for ideas about beauty and sexuality that do not correspond to nature: "Bizarre saint! Someone is contradicting you, and I am afraid that it is nature."[5] He does not think Christianity contains a shred of unity with the nature of the cosmos. He derides theists for their contradictions. He thinks the Jewish and Christian slave morality lacks practicality and obstructs will to power, the *Übermensch*, and the reevaluation of values. Equality poisons us and is impractical for society. For Nietzsche, theism's incapacity to explain the world with any accuracy throws it into nihilism. Therefore, to view Nietzsche through these unities foists no odd bias because he employs them. He implicitly values unity and its appeal to the fair-minded.

Understanding the Threefold Unity

The three beacons of worldview unity guide us with coherence, correspondence, and practicality.[6] Each expresses a different kind of harmony and qualities we seek as humans. We'll peer into Nietzsche's worldview from these three perspectives, each providing a focusing lens. I hope this approach and its strengths will resonate with you as fair-minded and sensible.

Coherence weighs the internal relationship between the essential claims of a worldview. The mind abhors contradictions. Does a worldview really accept itself? We look for serious inconsistencies where a worldview disrupts itself. This evaluation asks if a worldview applies its own principles to itself. Internal unity in the prime beliefs increases the appeal of a worldview through integrity.

Next, correspondence considers if a worldview measures up to the observable world. Can a worldview achieve unity with the perceived world both externally and internally? Does it agree with what we can see around us and inside of us? The external correspondence inquiry looks into a worldview's harmony with reality, the way it explains the external world. The internal correspondence inquiry explores our inner consciousness to determine if the claims of a worldview agree with our inner experience, consciousness, and awareness. We value a worldview's correspondence to outer and inner perception of reality.

Practicality, the third cornerstone of unity, studies how a worldview applies to the ongoing obligations necessary to live it out. Most people easily grasp the practicality aspect of worldview evaluation. Is it even possible to walk the talk of a worldview? Some ideas cannot possibly be practiced. Practicality greatly increases the appeal of a worldview because it means we can consistently commit to it in daily life. We desire to integrate a belief system into life, to hold it in good faith, and to authentically practice it without a false conscience. This may seem subjective, but it pertains to the rigors of daily life that Nietzsche appreciated.

Unity of Coherence in Nietzsche

Is a worldview consistent in its claims? Contradictions raise red flags. If a belief system contradicts itself, either explicitly or implicitly, common sense suspects a major problem. Explicit contradiction rarely occurs because the mind abhors rank conflicts. Implicit contradiction happens more often. Either way, the inner unity of the system disintegrates. We appeal to this when we say, "You can't have your cake and eat it too" or "The pot is calling the kettle black." Our desire for the unity of coherence also drives our universal disdain for hypocrisy, double standards, and injustice, and the high value we place on personal integrity. Hypocrisy may be a contradiction between moral standards we hold for others and for ourselves, or a contradiction between what we say and what we do. The failures of moral integrity in someone's actions upset us. The law of non-contradiction lies at the core of coherence. The law formally states that A cannot equal non-A at the same time, place, and in the same sense.

Implicit contradictions often hide from view and can be difficult to pinpoint. Explicit contradictions are easier to spot and are rare for a philosopher to commit. Either way, they signal problems. If a contradiction concerns a peripheral issue, then it may not corrupt the unity much and might be excused. However, if the contradiction involves key tenets of a thinker's system, then that equates to a major mechanical breakdown of a vehicle.

Nietzsche's inconsistencies appear to many observers, but a host of interpreters strive to reconcile his paradoxes. Attracting criticism for his contradictions, paradoxes, and confusions, Nietzsche does not seem concerned with such standards of sensibility. We can't know, but perhaps he wanted to provoke various interpretations. Remember that, for him, there are no bare facts, only interpretations of facts, only a unique perspective that sees facts through a little-understood grid of filters. He laughs when we try to pin him down. Most philosophers rigorously pursue unity in a worldview. In the end, Nietzsche does not.

On the positive side, Nietzsche merits applause for trying to be consistently atheist and intellectually honest. This stark honesty led him to difficult, though logical, conclusions. In addition to popularity for such honesty, it earns respect, even with people who deeply disagree with him. So he pursues a degree of coherence by following naturalistic assumptions to a logical conclusion. His atheism leads to an amoral ethic of power, survival, the abandonment of altruism, nihilism, and finally, to existential attempts to overcome all these concepts. He fully grasps that serious commitment to God's death leads to no objective morality, truth, or altruism. Nietzsche represents a form of atheism that won't sugarcoat the consequences of his worldview with altruism.

A paradox seems to contradict, but it may not. Nearly every major worldview contains some paradoxes. To the insider, a paradox contains subtleties and nuances of meaning that can be reconciled or eliminated by careful, often tedious, explanation and interpretation. This emic, or insider perspective, respects the epistemic right of worldview adherents to grasp their worldview with a subtlety that escapes outsiders. To outsiders looking in, a deep paradox glares out as a contradiction, a red flashing stoplight. This etic, or outsider perspective, comes from external observers. What appears as a contradiction to an outsider may be a paradox with subtle nuances of meaning and harmony to the insider, who reconciles that paradox with sophisticated measures.

Some critics may snicker that our attitude of fairness itself reflects Nietzsche's perspectivism. Postmodernists have long taken a perspectivist stance that there is no privileged position that allows truly objective analysis of the unities we seek. There are no privileged metanarratives. Nevertheless, even Nietzsche harshly criticized other worldviews and belief systems for their inconsistencies.

Nietzsche harbors many paradoxes, but entering into a full emic perspective that attempts to solve these paradoxes lies beyond our scope. Various schools of interpretation can try to unify a system of thought, or a thinker, by selecting an interpretive key from the clearer elements in a worldview. They then squeeze nonconforming elements to fit that chosen key. For example, Nazi interpreters selected a particular view of Nietzsche's *Übermensch* and a twisted view of will to power as their key. They forced the rest of Nietzsche's system through that keyhole. The mind naturally desires unity, so interpreters gravitate toward a forced unification of a vast system. This happens with many complex systems of thought from Plato to Freud. Moreover, fans understandably try to rid their favorite thinker of contradictions through the fancy footwork of nuanced interpretations that reconcile paradoxes.

We will avoid the errors of forcing unity or of disintegrating Nietzsche's natural unity. Instead of defending or attacking his paradoxes, we will identify some problem areas. A few major paradoxes to ponder in his system are will to power and *amor fati*; free will, morality, and herd ethics; eternal recurrence and free will; and epistemological relativism.

Will to Power and *Amor Fati*

No other paradox glares at observers of Nietzsche's worldview so intently as free will and determinism. In the passages where he speaks of will to power, Nietzsche emphasizes the power of the individual to wrestle life by the horns and dominate it. His triumphal tone prods us to be proactive and to shun all passivity. Reality shocks us when it dawns on us that we alone in the known universe can will. This voice in Nietzsche fuels an existential movement with persistent effects. You can choose. There's no excuse. Get up, get out there, and go change the world! The blank canvas of the world awaits your brushstrokes. However, another side of Nietzsche perplexes us about these claims.

He says you are entirely fated. Your choices are illusions determined by the unconscious forces of the cosmos. You are deluded by an inner world of illusions, and the ruse of that hallucination deceives you into thinking your will is free. Your will is moved by external forces and itself moves nothing. No mind causes your body to move. Everyone is captured by this illusion of volition. What's worse, the whole silly idea of volition and free will comes from those who concocted the idea to guilt you into submission. Free will is a control technique, a guilt trip. If there is no free will, there is no responsibility; if there is no responsibility, there is no guilt; if there is no guilt, there is no control.

Nietzsche's opposing combination of will and fate perplexes us. His triumphal will to power signifies nothing if will is an illusion. Nietzsche applauds those who practice *amor fati*, love of the fated nature of their lives. Your life is fated and all that occurred happened necessarily. This means your choices that you thought you chose freely were entirely a product of your circumstances. This supposedly positive confirmation of life looks like just giving up on everything—the good, the bad, and the ugly. After all, what happens in life must happen. Just roll with it. This paradox also casts shadows on morality, shifting moral choices into suspicion. Are these two central tenets of Nietzsche's worldview coherent?

Free Will, Morality, and Herd Ethics

Nietzsche's astonishing teaching of will to power earns him both praise and scorn, both love and contempt. The lack of clarity about the concept enabled some to interpret the teaching for political oppression. The Nazis' hijacking of the idea blighted Nietzsche's reputation for many decades. Despite this, later existential thinkers positively interpreted Nietzsche's will to power and overman as exultations in human potential for improvement.

Does Nietzsche's will to power mean that I have free will? In all likelihood, no. No source for free will exists in Nietzsche's worldview where we are fated and have no choice, yet he still urges us to seize control and power. The will to power in us necessarily rises up to act due to our evolutionary nature and is synonymous with our drive to survive, especially since instinctual action fits Nietzsche's amorality. As he said, "Life is will to power," and what we do we must, and we must seek power in every sense of the word. There is no right or wrong. For Nietzsche, morality at best is egoism, the individual acting out of self-interest. The amorality of a deterministic will to power harmonizes well enough with egoism.

An internal conflict created by Nietzsche's attack on herd morality weakens his coherence. Weak masses of people collectively bind their wee powers to overpower strong people. Exploiting guilt and shame, the weak masses develop herd morals out of an innate instinct, a new strategy in their collective will to power. Herds cooperate to overpower those that would oppress them. If they employ guilt and shame to get power, they still seek will to power. After all, the weak do what they innately must, having no free will. A ferocious lion corners the herd, so they stampede the lion. How is this not a collective will to power? On a human scale, we see this frequently with democratic masses overpowering abusive forces of the strong in their society. This might be legislative, but the masses also use moralizing guilt-trips and shaming techniques. Consider how contemporary special interest groups manipulate victimhood as a ploy for power. If we are not free, and we do what we must by seeking power, then the herd moralists have found a way to expand their power.

Moreover, on Nietzsche's analysis, the herd operates according to *instinct*, yet he consistently praises those who act on predatory instincts instead of reason. The herd's instinct for self-protection evolves into traditional morals. He hates that herd instinct turned into morality and praises master morality and exploitation. Master morality too originates from instinct. For all of Nietzsche's explanatory theory of morality, it is not clear why the slave morality is inferior. After all, the weak merely found a way to pool their power together to overpower the strong. The weak combine their will to power for protection. Why is this bad? Nietzsche might retort that it keeps the human species from rising to the superhuman level of the *Übermensch*. Yet no reason clearly emerges about why evolving is preferable. Even if the entire human species suffered extinction today, there is no reason that this is bad in a valueless worldview. Our extinction may enable survival for many other species that we are killing off. That we are the highest and most sophisticated creatures presents no justification and is a prejudice.

Eternal Recurrence and Free Will

The paradox of eternal recurrence halts many readers with a stupendous vision. The concept is not perfectly clear, but it shifts the importance to the here and now, not the eternal afterlife of theistic religions. Does Nietzsche literally believe eternal recurrence will take place on a cosmic scale? Or should we merely live *as if* it will and thus transform our demeanor? Either way, the idea leaves one with deeper conundrums. If Nietzsche teaches that recurrence is literal, then essentially I am currently living one lifespan of an infinite series. This means an infinite series of my whole life has already occurred. Another infinite series will occur in the future. Of course I carry no personal memories from one life to the next, nor am I aware of any of the previous lives. Aside from the serious problems of actual infinites occurring, there is a clash with what this doctrine is supposed to do. If I must live this life repeatedly, then I have already lived it many times. How could I live any differently in this life than I have in past lives, since everything must recur precisely the same? How could this possibly transform how I live now? I can't change anything about my choices or myself. Such a revelation compels me to fatalism and destroys my free will. *Que será, será.* Whatever will be, will be; whatever has been, will be again. Perhaps Nietzsche means that this life is the first of an endless series. Nothing indicates that, nor could he possibly know it.

Did Nietzsche believe in a figurative doctrine of eternal recurrence, a kind of self-help technique for guiding life? If no actual recurrence happens, then we must trick ourselves into a better life by pretending it will. Perhaps that would snap us into a clearer perspective. Aside from things beyond our control, we do choose many things we would not ever want to repeat. How practical would decision-making be if I knew that recurrence was imaginary and that life is really a one-shot deal? A simpler method would be to ask myself if I am truly certain I want to do something. Why am I certain I want it? Don't wander through life being tossed around by everything, but be purposeful. If you constantly second-guess, you end in a weak life of indecision.

Relativity of Epistemology

Epistemology forms a serious part of any worldview. A theory of how people acquire knowledge intertwines with everything. A worldview claims at least some tenets about the world. To construct a worldview, you must implicitly claim to know something true.

A paradox arises when Nietzsche explicitly claims tenets about the way the world is, about human nature, about morality, and about the eternal return, but relativizes all claims of factual knowledge. He affirms that truth is worth no more than appearance, that there are no facts or absolute truths, that truth is really a construct of the will, and that interpretations overrule imaginary facts. When navigating his claims we should remember that if knowledge arises from the will to power of someone, then he envelops his claims in that statement. His claims too must arise as will to power. If any of his famous ideas accurately explain human experience, they ostensibly are factual. Yet he undermines his claims by teaching that ultimately all truth claims are constructs. If correct, then this claim is itself a will to truth.

If there are no facts, then there are no facts in his system of ideas. We could stop here, but the implications continue. If there are no facts in his system and all is a matter of interpretations driven by his will to power, then I should be wary of accepting any of it as true or accurate. Skeptics can be doctrinaire about their skepticism, dogmatically insisting that there is no truth. Postmodernists claim that no metanarrative rules over all narratives, but that too is a metanarrative about all metanarratives. Perspectivists claim to have the correct perspective on truth. Such ironies should not escape us.

We have explored a few, but not all, problem areas that upset the unifying coherence of Nietzsche's worldview: will to power and *amor fati*; the determinism of eternal recurrence and free will; free will, morality, and herd ethics; and epistemological relativism. Now we will examine some areas of concern in Nietzsche's unity of correspondence.

Unity of Correspondence in Nietzsche

We inherently value the unity of correspondence in a worldview. Does a worldview's central claims correspond with reality? Does it fit with the way things really are? As a simple example, if I claim, "It is pouring rain in downtown Boston at 9:00 a.m., October 8, 2015," then this is true if it actually was raining in Boston at that time. On a more serious level, if a materialistic worldview claims that nothing outside of physical matter exists, we must ask if this claim matches up with reality.

This unity test appeals to plain common sense: a view of the world must fit the obvious and plainly observable facts. However, commonsensical as it sounds, complications arise. The correspondence theory of truth underlies this test. This truth theory appeals especially to the scientific mind-set in our age. Many of us employ scientific methods in our careers and daily lives. We seek empirical evidence for truth claims, and we think it is irresponsible to accept ideas without sufficient evidence. To know things empirically means to know them though sensory experiences. A few people accept only scientific evidence for truth claims, a position sometimes called scientism or positivism. Pretty simple. Now for the complications.

Nietzsche and the postmodern movement that would later lionize him may not readily agree with the correspondence test. How can anyone reliably know the world as it really is using empirical evidence? What we call facts rests on interpretations of observations. Observed facts filter through a maze of assumptions, prejudices, rough estimates, and murky associations we don't fully understand. Those assumptions precede observation, guide them, and do not proceed from them. Indeed, the widely accepted notion that true knowledge must originate from science alone is an unproven assumption. Perhaps many people assume it and perhaps it is a reasonable assumption, but it is still an assumption. At the very least, that claim did not come from science, for there is no empirical evidence for it. *Apriori* assumptions guide *aposteriori* observations.[7] Brute facts cannot be accessed directly. When we think we can know, we assume our rational faculties and our senses accurately mediate the world to our minds. As it turns out, our rational faculties and senses notoriously snag on glitches. Our epistemic ability is a telescope with human—all too human—fingerprints smudging the lens.

Contemporary scientific methods strive to eliminate these human glitches and dig down to the bare facts that correspond with reality. The historical landscape of science is littered with many abandoned buildings of false theories once thought to be true. The self-correcting wheels of scientific progress grind slowly and might reverse at times. After bitter struggles with each other over how to interpret the facts they gather, scientific communities reach a consensus. Operative words: community and consensus. Nietzsche would jaw-lock on these like a starving wolf as he howls that truth is a function of will to power, a communal construction of truth.

In addition, scientific communities differ in methods. Scientific methods differ from field to field. No one end-all method for science exists. The vaunted double-blind placebo-controlled method works for some medical studies but won't work in other fields of science. Some fields require repeatable experiments that reasonably predict outcomes and explain why, but other fields can only engage in observation. Yet for all of its problems, science and the correspondence theory of truth dominate today as the way to understand the nature of things. Does Nietzsche's worldview correspond to reality? We will look at two of his ideas: eternal recurrence and determinism.

Eternal Recurrence

Will you eternally relive your life? Does such a view correspond with reality? Cosmology today simply cannot affirm this. Little evidence exists for this claim, making any chance for correspondence remote. The sequence of physical events in the history of the cosmos would have to be precisely the same for another 13.8 billion years, the estimated age of the universe. For this to happen, the cosmos may have to collapse and expand again. Few take Nietzsche's idea as a serious possibility but rather see it as a metaphor for analyzing one's life. Some current multiverse cosmology theories claim that infinite parallel universes probably exist, which if true would make Nietzsche's eternal return conceivable. Can these contemporary theories confirm Nietzsche's eternal recurrence? We'll look at the multiverse cosmology further below.

Deterministic Human Nature

While Nietzsche believes we can control our actions, he thinks we cannot control what we desire. There is no ground for responsibility because we cannot do other than what we do. His position hovers around the compatibilist view of free will. We can think of it as a soft determinism, but *amor fati* in a materialist cosmos sounds like a hard determinism. Does Nietzsche's determinist view of human nature correspond to reality? Scientifically, or externally, we have no way to know, despite brain and neuroscience research. The perennial nut of free will refuses to be cracked this way. Intuitively we know that we control ourselves and choose actions. Most of us certainly live as if we could have chosen differently in most situations. We hold ourselves genuinely responsible for our choices on this ability basis. Without such responsibility, society would hardly function. We intuitively perceive our inner ability to intentionally choose, and we are acutely aware that we actually choose. Does Nietzsche's theory of illusory free will correspond to our inner awareness? Powerful inner awareness and consciousness present a psychological reality that we cannot ignore, and determinism does not correspond to this inner reality. Science has not shown—perhaps it cannot—whether people are free or determined, or to what extent. However, nearly universal internal experience tells us we can freely choose.

The unity of correspondence in Nietzsche's worldview suffers disruption. His key doctrines of eternal recurrence and his determinism struggle to correspond with reality. Next we examine the unity of practice in his work.

Unity of Practice in Nietzsche

Does Nietzsche's worldview work in a practical sense? Can it close the gap between its theory and daily practice? Worldviews should not have logical disconnects between theory and practice. Here we ponder whether someone thoroughly committed to his vision could live it out consistently. Some worldviews may be beautiful, intriguing, or enthralling but impossible to practice. Some things work for one but not for another. We might quip the cliché "It works for me!" so that nobody can argue. Practicality may appear to be a highly subjective standard of measurement relative to each person, but some ideas put into practice can become unworkable for anyone.

At first Nietzsche might appear practical. He inspires and influences many across the spectrum of the arts and culture. However, the practicality question asks whether a specific idea would create an absurd and unlivable life if someone committed to live it out *consistently*. If ideas carry consequences, those consequences will emerge in practice.

A follower of Nietzsche's worldview would fall into a few practical quagmires if he or she seriously committed to the following views: determinism, ethical egoism, eternal recurrence, and epistemological relativism. We have seen some of these ideas earlier, but now we examine them for their impact on lives.

Determinism

Considering Nietzsche's determinism yet again, is it livable and practical? Nietzsche might ask, "Practical for whom?" Just because a worldview "doesn't work for me" doesn't mean it won't work for others. Live and let live! While a person may theoretically subscribe to determinism, is it possible to live as if all human actions follow a preset course? The problems that arise from determinism dizzy the mind to its limits.

In Nietzsche's worldview nothing exists to allow free will. My actions cannot be otherwise than what they are because I *necessarily* perform all actions. Driven by uncontrolled internal physics that defy analysis, from every finger twitch to marriage to education, all that occurs internally follows deterministically from one state to the next. If this is so, the implications stretch into every area of life. We have already seen that this presents problems with coherence and correspondence, but now it hits home in practice. Meaning and responsibility vanish. Even will to power can't escape this black hole.

Merit and demerit, praise and blame, the noble and the criminal all evaporate. Nietzsche knew all distinctions disappear, and he explicitly promotes this. Action fades to meaninglessness, plunging us into a nihilistic abyss. His idea of will to power goads us to leap over the abyss by urging us to act instinctively in our self-interest. His doctrine of the eternal recurrence also presses us to act as if we will walk down this same path of life again. We should walk down a path that leads to our joy. How, as a chance product of a deterministic cosmos, and forever in the clenches of that process, can I have any input into the course of my life? Nietzsche shrugs. This paradox leads to an unlivable commitment. Could I survive twenty-four hours of life like this? It isn't clear that he himself lived this way. We cannot extract meaningful life out of the nonexistent ether of choice. If I earnestly attempted to do what Nietzsche taught, not only would it be impossible with the tools he says I have, but it would not be fulfilling. Nihilism reigns.

Ethical Egoism

Nietzsche's ethical egoism creates practical snags. Will to power reverses all values and virtues to form the core of this amoral ethic. In his egoistic lifestyle, we should act in self-interest. We should not live for others or sacrifice ourselves for others. Nietzsche's imperative would be to act according to the principle of self-interest such that you could wish that this act would recur eternally. Could a person follow this as a normative ethic? Normative ethics inform us what a person *should* do. As an egoist, I would not even want to tell others to act in their self-interest. If they did, they would use will to power over me. I would have to tell others they should treat me however they wish as long as they use me to their advantage. Thus, egoism must remain a secret to work, but ironically it tells people how they should act.

If I am to maximize my power and control over my world, I suffer great disadvantage by telling others to do the same. Thieves don't prey on other thieves, but on the honest. No thief would tell everyone to start stealing, for his or her ethic depends on others' honesty. Will to power can't be universalized without emasculating the idea into mere self-help and self-mastery. How useful is this ethic, and is it possible to consistently practice? Personal application seems impossible, and if everyone did it, anarchy may ensue. Some efforts have been made to revitalize Nietzsche and tone down his egoistic will to power into a self-improvement project of self-overcoming. This rehabilitates Nietzsche and perhaps saves a critical part of his doctrine, but this decaffeinated brew misses his full intent.

Eternal Recurrence

Eternal recurrence says to live as if your life will recur eternally. If I consistently commit to this, it creates an unworkable scenario, whether I truly believe it as a cosmology or merely pretend. If I truly believe, I must think my lifetime resembles a number in an infinite string of numbers. I have no idea how many lifetimes precede this one or how many follow it. Indeed, there has to be an infinite series in both directions. Moreover, any iteration of life precisely replicates all preceding lives. The psychological state this would create numbs us with fatalism, perhaps even paralyzing action. This isn't even karma, which says each life occurrence contains rewards and punishments carried over from a past life. Might this belief even promote intense nihilism? Some may choose to end this life if it becomes unbearable? Like a video game, they press restart—only to play the same game over.

Suppose that I merely pretend *as if* my life will recur, but I know it won't. Is this practically feasible? Concerning eternal recurrence, Heller says,

> Yet the metaphysical nonsense of these contradictory doctrines is not entirely lacking in poetic and didactic method. The Eternal Recurrence of All Things is Nietzsche's mythic formula of a meaningless world, the universe of nihilism, and the *Übermensch* stands for its transcendence.[8]

The overman alone can stomach eternal recurrence as some acid-test of tenacity. For us mere mortals, eternal recurrence as a coping mechanism could urge us to be more thoughtful and careful, invigorating our appreciation of this life. Such a self-deception only works if we really believed it and became delusional. However, perhaps reality sets in upon the premature death of someone we know. Nihilistic emotions and thoughts run rampant. Maybe YOLO is true. What happened to hammer-smashing idols? Is the eternal return another delusion? Can such a strategy be practically sustained and truly lived with full commitment?

Epistemological Relativism

Nietzsche's will to knowledge also leads to practical difficulties. For him all knowledge emanates from individuals or cultures. No transcultural or transpersonal truth exists because all claims of truth are perspectival, and knowledge from one perspective may not harmonize with knowledge from another perspective. What someone claims as truth is merely a matter of perspective, opinion, or interpretation. We warp, distort, and selectively narrow facts so much that there is no way to access the actual truth, even with scientific methods that fall prey to the same problems.

Science is merely another perspective. Objective truth eludes us. All facts are mediated and interpreted from perspectives.

Can this view be sincerely maintained and put into practice? The abandonment of objective truth earmarks our contemporary time and many would agree with Nietzsche. Those today who assume the relativity of truth seem to function well enough, but do they accept the full-strength dose of the skeptical state of mind that ensues? If they do, they doubt all truth claims and shun dogmatisms, wherever they come from.

Healthy skepticism typifies an educated person. In a world rife with rhetoric, politics, special interest groups, sales pitches, and hucksters, we quickly wise up to how easily "facts and statistics" get distorted. *Caveat emptor.* If we are to discern shams, we can't abandon the idea of truth altogether. We discern better the distortion of facts with the discovery of the unvarnished truth. We detect the selective deletion of inconvenient facts because we can see other relevant facts. Counterfeits become obvious when we know the authentic. We must humbly accept that we err in judgment and that no one is always right. Facts can and will be manipulated. The detection of deception becomes easier when we maintain that truth exists.

Epistemological relativism faces another practical challenge. If we sincerely believe that truth varies according to individual subjectivity, then this fact itself must vary too. This is a failure to be consistently committed. Ironically, radical relativists like Nietzsche dogmatically claim their ideas as if they are immune to the illusions everyone else harbors. This qualifies as a breach of common sense, as we saw above. We can't bridge the logical chasm between Nietzsche's theoretical claim and daily life practice.

We navigate life's waters hoping the navigation charts represent factual knowledge, but we also remain vigilant. Trust but verify. We scan for errors of contradiction. If two maps explicitly contradict, then either one or both are wrong. We also search for correspondence. We know observable reality can be accurately stated. When an island exists exactly where the map claims, we have correspondent truth. With good maps, we can practically live. These three unities value some worldview quality. Next we look at the completeness of Nietzsche's naturalism.

CHAPTER 10

Nietzsche and Naturalism

Does a worldview need to be comprehensive? A comprehensive worldview integrates more and enhances the desirability of a worldview with a high *quantity* of unity. Humanity insatiably yearns to understand. As our knowledge grows rapidly, a worldview must be scalable, affording longevity and growth to itself. A worldview should explain most of the important aspects of the world because this engenders more confidence and satisfaction than one that explains less. Imagine a perfectly coherent, correspondent, and practical worldview that includes all known knowledge. It would surpass others in explanatory capacity and power. However, the world is a moving target that encompasses a vast ocean of experience and knowledge.

To illustrate why worldviews need to expand, imagine that intelligent aliens landed on Earth tomorrow. Would you adapt your worldview to incorporate that new and rather important knowledge? Would aliens turn your worldview upside down? Would you ignore them? Eventually, if you did not explain this new knowledge, your worldview would pass into obsolescence, lacking reasonable completeness. Gaps of explanatory capacity weaken worldviews and risk implosion. This is why Nietzsche believed God died. In a post-Darwin age God explains nothing. Thus, many old worldviews have died. Nietzsche thinks all theistic worldviews run this dead-end path.

As we peer back to Nietzsche we must remember that knowledge then looked more like a pond than an ocean. We cannot anachronistically hold Nietzsche responsible for what we know today or fault past thinkers for ignorance of recent developments. We can't quite estimate Nietzsche himself on explanatory capacity looking at today's knowledge. Yet we can reflect on the naturalistic worldview arising since Nietzsche that many contemporary atheists share.

Reflections on Nietzsche, Minds, and Naturalism

From the perspective of naturalism, the rise of consciousness, rationality, and will in a material cosmos causes some deep concerns. Nietzsche rejects as illusions three core beliefs most of us firmly believe: "People projected their three 'inner facts' out of themselves and onto the world— the facts they believed in most fervently, the will, the mind, and the I."[1] We fabricate our concept of being from our fictional "I." Thus, "the 'inner world' is full of illusions: the will is one of them." These three beliefs do not fit into a naturalistic worldview, and Nietzsche must redefine them as surface phenomena of consciousness. Scientific knowledge of the brain and neural function advances daily, yet the rise of these fascinating realities and abilities troubles even contemporary research. Some agree with Nietzsche. Intelligence incorporates high-level complexities and abilities such as language; the ability to create new ideas, transfer that complex information between minds, develop logic and mathematics; and increasingly sophisticated scientific investigation. If someone presupposes that matter alone exists, then these functions must arise from matter alone and operate under the control of physical laws. These abilities can't rise above their ground. Thus naturalists often follow their materialistic assumption to the logical conclusion that these three inner realities create illusions. In doing so, Nietzsche leads as their predecessor.

Friedrich Nietzsche @TwilightOfIdols
How did reason come into the world? As is fitting, in an irrational manner, by accident.[2]

The presence of reason, consciousness, and free will burdens a naturalistic worldview's completeness. Nietzsche assumes Darwin, evolution, and the existence of empirical knowledge. In this tweet, he thinks reason arises in nature as a fluke. Reason arose accidentally just like life itself. To arrive at rational creatures in naturalism, the cosmos must accidentally cross three thresholds: the threshold of nothing to something, the threshold of matter to living creatures, and the threshold of living organisms to human rational beings.

The first threshold lies at the beginning in an expansion of energy from nothing, the Big Bang. In the naturalistic worldview, the vast size of the universe started from nothing and was caused by nothing. New theories of a quantum vacuum will be discussed below. Though Nietzsche knew nothing about the Big Bang, the prevailing contemporary view among naturalists says that nothing produced everything. For many centuries atheists, including Nietzsche, believed that matter existed eternally. However, we now know that the universe began at some specific place and time about 13.8 billion years ago. The rapid expansion began from an infinitesimal point smaller than an atom. While many scientists accept a beginning of the universe, naturalists often claim that absolutely nothing caused this epic moment. A difference between Nietzschean and contemporary naturalism is that Nietzsche held the cosmos as eternal, but contemporaries usually embrace the Big Bang arising out of nothing. Either way, there is no cause or God.

The second threshold of explanatory capacity that naturalism must cross involves the inception of life from nonliving matter. Atheists assert that life emerged from nonliving matter. Scientific method begins with a hypothesis. To support the hypothesis, either an experiment with a predictable and repeatable outcome must be created, or a set of data must come from careful observation that is open to others. Though Stanley Miller and later scientists including Carl Sagan have tried to recreate life from non-living matter, no one has come anywhere near creating an experiment that generates life from non-living matter alone. Such an experiment faces enormous obstacles.

The other possible path to knowledge in science involves observations. NASA today believes life emerges from nonliving matter and seeks to prove it through observational science.[3] It explores new worlds and finds exoplanets outside our solar system in the "goldilocks zone" revolving around their suns. In our quest to explore space we hope to find extraterrestrial life. This quest assumes that life can arise from nonliving stuff. No one has ever observed such life emerging. If someone could observe even single-cell organisms emerging from nonliving matter, then we cross the second threshold. The naturalistic worldview, which claims science as its method, has no basis in experimental or observational methods to claim that life emerged from nonliving matter. Like extraterrestrial life, life from nonliving matter has never been observed. Nor has life ever been recreated experimentally. Thus, life from matter alone is a massive assumption in naturalism.

Some will casually dismiss the assumption as insignificant because few if any options exist. A worldview's assumptions color its character, and naturalism today assumes that knowledge emerges from scientific methods alone. While Nietzsche distrusts the values driving positivistic science, we see from his tweet above that he assumes life just accidentally happened. Even 120 years later, naturalists agree and are unable to offer evidence. The incongruence between a chosen scientific epistemology and the assumption of life's origin raises concerns. Naturalism's life assumption attains coherence with some other aspects of its materialism. However, naturalism seeks knowledge through empirical correspondence. Thus, Nietzsche's and naturalism's beliefs about life's inception disturb the unity of their worldview and correspond to no observed reality. In short, naturalists insist on evidence but have none to prove life arose from crude matter alone.

A worldview that primarily relies on correspondence and critiques other worldviews for not doing so raises concerns. Does naturalism specially plead for a pass on the origin of life to keep the worldview coherent, hoping nobody notices it violates its own epistemology? It fails to explain the origin of life in its own desired terms. Its explanatory capacity suffers because the inception of life from pure matter must happen before evolution, rationality, and consciousness. The incremental steps from single-celled organisms to rational and conscious human life assumes life's inception.

The third explanatory threshold that naturalism must cross involves the emergence of human rationality and consciousness. In naturalism these high-order human traits must incrementally evolve out of nonrational and nonconscious matter. Rocks don't have brains, but in naturalism's view, rocks gave birth to brains over billions of years. Darwinian evolution claims that over time, life complexity increased via natural selection, and life evolved from simple one-celled organisms to rational and conscious human life. Granting this is the case, we can have no confidence in anyone's rational abilities. I retweet Nietzsche: "Reason comes . . . in an irrational manner, by accident." Rationality from nonrational matter undermines any ability to know truth and rests on unstable grounds. Ironically, Nietzsche understood this. The survival of a species depends not on rationality or truth-knowing abilities but will to power. He grasped that assuming naturalism's view that human reason arose from nonreason, our rational abilities are not trustworthy to find truth. Knowledge disintegrates. We can't trust our minds, and our ability to do science fails. Nietzsche knew this feedback loop leads to nihilism and tried to escape its vortex through will. Abandon the shipwreck of truth and knowledge and leap into the sea of will. Yet we can wonder if he willed us to truly believe that there is no truth, only will. The pungent irony shouldn't escape us.

Consciousness and freedom evade us for similar reasons in naturalism because consciousness must arise from nonconscious and nonfree determined matter and energy. If consciousness arose by random occurrences, then it too becomes illusory. A consciousness produced by random forces could not be a reliable mind for knowing truth. Any hope of free will also depends on consciousness because free will requires awareness. To avoid the puzzles of consciousness and freedom, Nietzsche abandoned them as illusions. Is this practical? Intentional activity vanishes. Can the philosopher who says consciousness is an illusion do so without truly assuming consciousness? The pretense that some know as a fact that consciousness and free will are illusions indicates that they believe they are not under an illusion. Naysayers of consciousness assume what they deny. Thus, another irony.

The recent story of one famous philosophical naturalist and atheist is relevant here. Antony Flew, who for some thirty years led global atheism, abandoned his philosophical naturalism due to difficulties like those above. This brought him much scorn from many atheists. Recounting a key truth and realization that prompted his departure from atheism, Flew tells the story of the typing monkeys.

Flew, Schroeder, and Typing Monkeys

For decades atheists have insisted that order and design in the cosmos could emerge randomly. If this was so, then human DNA could arise randomly. If human DNA could arise randomly from matter, then rationality and consciousness would follow. An analogy of monkeys often accompanied this claim of random order of complexity. If some monkeys were given typewriters, eventually, with enough time, their random typing could produce a Shakespearean play, like *Hamlet*. Some researchers tested this, placing a typewriter in a cage with six monkeys. After a month the monkeys typed fifty pages, yet without even typing one single word, not even the word "a." Flew recounts Gerhard Schroeder's calculation of the odds of typing even a single Shakespearean sonnet:

> All sonnets are the same length. They're by definition fourteen lines long. I picked . . . "Shall I compare thee to a summer's day?" I counted the number of letters . . . 488. What's the likelihood of hammering away and getting 488 letters in the exact sequence as in "Shall I Compare Thee to a Summer's Day?"? What you end up with is 26 multiplied by itself 488 times—or 26 to the 488th power. Or . . . in base 10, 10 to the 690th.

[Now] the number of particles in the universe—not grains of sand, I'm talking about protons, electrons, and neutrons, is 10 to the 80th. Ten to the 80th is 1 with 80 zeros after it. Ten to the 690th is 1 with 690 zeros after it. There are not enough particles in the universe to write down the trials; you'd be off by a factor of 10 to the 600th.

If you took the entire universe and converted it to computer chips—forget the monkeys—each one weighing a millionth of a gram and had each computer chip able to spin out 488 trials at, say, a million times a second; if you turn the entire universe into these microcomputer chips and these chips were spinning a million times a second [producing] random letters, the number of trials you would get since the beginning of time would be 10 to the 90th trials. It would be off again by a factor of 10 to the 600th. You would never get a sonnet by chance. Yet the world just thinks the monkeys can do it every time.[4]

Flew remarks that if naturalism's theorem of order by random chance can't produce a sonnet, then to think the universe could produce the infinitely more complex organisms of life plunges into sheer absurdity.[5] Human DNA contains 3.1 billion base pairs in one molecule. If the universe cannot produce a mere poem of 488 letters of information, then creating DNA with 3.1 billion base pairs of information by random ordering or self-organization exhausts all credulity. This realization ended Flew's lifelong devotion to atheistic materialism. He became a theist. However, naturalists have a new theory to explain just how our universe could perform the impossible: the multiverse. Remember, Nietzsche knew nothing about these debates, but they attempt to solve challenges in the naturalist worldview he championed.

Multiverses and Random Organization

Multiverse theories hope to explain how random organization could create life. At least nine multiverse theories compete, mostly arising from innovative quantum physics and M-theory.[6] A fantastic range of possible worlds and scenarios emerges. Suppose an atheist grants that our local universe alone does not have enough time or chance organizations to create life. Multiverse theories offer more time and chances with infinite local universes. With an infinity of universes, at least one would fabricate the complex organization of matter required for life. It just so happens that you are in *that* universe now. That's why we can even discuss it. Aren't we lucky? Our luck in this Multi-MegaCosmic lottery resembles winning a bet that upon rolling a quintillion dice at once every cube will turn up the number five—on the first roll! However, if you can roll the dice an infinite number of times, eventually the combination will happen. In fact, it will happen over and over infinitely. Boom. Eternal recurrence.

If an infinity of universes exists, then we can imagine ourselves in a Nietzschean eternal recurrence, or even a simultaneous occurrence. Anything that is *possible* is *actual* in some far-flung universe. The multiverse remains speculative, but scientists strive to prove which theory is correct.

Perhaps corroborating evidence will come, but even enthusiastic proponents admit it will be difficult. I remain open to the possibility, but the rational contortions to accept this picture render it implausible. How much evidence do we need to believe a multiverse corresponds to reality? Let's generously imagine that a multiverse gains credibility. Even if true, materialistic naturalism inherits the same philosophical problems it faces with a single universe.

The infinite regress problem remains. Either the multiverse began to exist, or it exists eternally. If it began to exist, it must have a cause. Anything that begins existing is caused, including the multiverse. An infinite regress of causation problem remains. On the other hand, if the multiverse exists eternally, it encounters the same challenges this cosmology endured for thousands of years. Infinite physical series cannot be empirically demonstrated, only theorized or assumed. Even advocates admit that empirical verification of the multiverse lies beyond reach, but theoretically the multiverse may be coherent. Thus the coherency of the multiverse lies in its assumption of eternal materialism. As provocative as the current wardrobe of multiverse theories may be, they are shiny new overcoats layered on the age-old metaphysical dress of cosmology.

Nietzsche knew nothing of a multiverse, but his eternal recurrence suggests a remarkably parallel idea and outcome. If the multiverse proves true, his eternal return may gain more than plausibility. It may be necessary. Contemporary naturalism shares the same materialistic assumptions, resulting in similar cosmologies. Eternality of the cosmos will be safe to assume again, because unlike our local universe that we know had a beginning, the multiverse lies beyond most scientific investigation. The multiverse rehabilitates naturalism's cosmology and Nietzsche's eternal return. Yet, as we explored above, two of the three threshold crossings remain. A multiverse worldview supplies no reason to trust rationality, consciousness, or free will. They remain illusory, as Nietzsche said. If the multiverse is true, a multinihilism ensues, or rather, some "nihiliverse." Nietzsche remains relevant, though the nihilism he hoped to overcome looms multiplied, if not infinite. His solutions endure unchanged.

Here Nietzsche earns a claim to fame. Even if we reject his conclusions, we can learn from him the values of tenacity and intellectual honesty. Seeing materialistic naturalism's logical conclusions, he honestly faces the impossible confidence in human reason, consciousness, and search for knowledge. Epistemological nihilism ensues, with moral nihilism following. Therefore, he tracks naturalism to its consistent conclusion that without rational truth all that is left is Dionysian instincts driving will to power. In his tragic life he would resolutely remake himself over and over. Chasing a Sisyphean feat, he willed to power his *amor fati* riding an eternal cosmic carousel until vertigo consumed him.

From Nietzsche's very last sentence in his last book, *Ecce Homo*, this last tweet unveils a great thrust of his life, a culmination of his efforts and identity. He identifies himself with Dionysus, the ancient Greek god of the passions, fertility, wine, and revelry. The values and principles of Dionysus oppose Christ's life and message, and Nietzsche sees himself as an incarnation of Dionysus. As he pens these words the ink runs dry in his prolific pen. In Turin, on January 3, 1889, Nietzsche witnesses a cart horse suffer a merciless whipping. Lurching to sympathetically embrace the wretched horse, he collapses into a mental breakdown as an unknown philosopher. His last twelve years of life slip into an eclipsed penumbra of insanity just as his popularity volcanically erupts to legendary levels. His history grows into legend until his death in 1900, and since then his legend springs into myth among a pantheon of philosophers.

Friedrich Nietzsche @TwilightOfIdols

—Have I been understood?—*Dionysus against the crucified one . . .*[7] #occupywilltopower

Glossary

This glossary of terms will help readers find a concise definition of difficult words and concepts in *Tweetable Nietzsche* to aid comprehension of ideas.

amoralism: the idea that human action is not good or evil in any way.

amor fati: love of fate, especially the specific order of every determined event in one's life.

aposteriori **(knowledge):** knowledge that arises only from and is dependent upon experience, or knowledge that requires experience.

apriori **(knowledge):** knowledge that precedes experience or is independent of experience, or knowledge that does not require experience.

Aristotle: (384–322 BCE) Greek philosopher and most famous student of Plato, though his ideas differed. Aristotle employed a more empirical approach to knowledge. He contributed enormously to Western culture and philosophy by pioneering many academic disciplines.

atheism: the belief that no God exists.

atheist: someone who believes no God exists and that no evidence exists for God.

atom: in ancient atomism, the smallest possible piece of matter. Atoms are tiny spheres of matter that cannot be divided.

Bonhoeffer, Dietrich: (1906–1945) Lutheran pastor, theologian, and martyr whose short life deeply influenced Christian theology.

categorical imperative: in Kant's thought, this universal moral rule sums up the entire moral duty that every person should follow regardless of the circumstances or the outcome. The categorical imperative says one should act according to the principle that one could wish that all people universally follow.

coherence: as a theory of truth, coherence within a system of claims or beliefs makes something true. A system that contains no contradictions has high coherence and truth-value.

compatibilism: the idea that both free will and determinism can be reconciled and made compatible with each other. A particular man does what he most desires, but he does not control or choose his desires.

correspondence: as a theory of truth, correspondence with observable facts makes claims true. A claim or system that corresponds with observable evidence grants truth-value.

deduction: (adj., deductive) a process of reasoning that starts with a general conclusion or law that applies to every example.

demythologization: the practice of eliminating anything related to the supernatural from a text or story.

deontology: an ethical theory based upon duty which says moral acts are required regardless of their consequences. Kant's ethical system is the best-known deontology.

Descartes, René: (1596–1650) French rationalist philosopher, mathematician, and father of modernity. He revolutionized the search for knowledge beyond all doubt by using doubt to find the indubitable axiom of knowledge in *cogito ergo sum* (I think, therefore I exist).

determinism: the idea that people are part of nature and controlled by natural laws both externally and internally, such that they must do what they do. Divine determinism holds that God wholly determines the actions of people, either directly or through the laws of nature God ordained.

Dionysus: the Greek god of ecstasy, revelry, drunkenness, and orgiastic pleasure.

egoism: an ethical theory based upon self-interest and self-preservation, though it may include enlightened self-interest that includes moral acts toward others.

empiricism: the idea that all knowledge arises from or out of sensory experience and not from rational concepts that precede experience.

Enlightenment: a powerful movement of the eighteenth century that promoted science, reason, liberalism, and naturalism. It opposed the church and looked harshly upon many Christian beliefs.

epistemology: the field of philosophy that studies the nature and extent of knowledge and truth, as well as how to attain them.

Epicurus: (c. 340–270 BCE) Greek philosopher, atomist, and hedonist who taught *ataraxia,* or tranquility of the body and mind during turbulent times.

eternal recurrence: Nietzsche's conception of the endless repetition of all events in the precise order in which they have occurred in the past.

ethics: the study of moral principles and values and whether they are normative.

existentialism: a worldview that promotes the existence of the individual above and beyond knowledge and science. The intuitive self-awareness of being precedes and drives all other concerns.

ex nihilo: out of nothing, from nothing.

fascism: a totalitarian political scheme putting the state in total control of individuals, social institutions, religion, and business.

Freud, Sigmund: (1856–1939) founder of the psychoanalytic approach to psychology.

hedonism: the ethical theory that says humans should pursue pleasure to attain happiness.

Heraclitus: (c. 540–475 BCE) Greek philosopher from Ephesus who taught atomism and the philosophy of change.

hermeneutics: the field of interpreting texts, or of interpreting the meaning of human existence.

hermeneutics of suspicion: interpretation of any form of discourse that assumes and looks for the projection of power over others through manipulation.

individualism: the view that the individual person is the center of politics and all human concerns. In all concerns such as political organization, morality, or knowledge, the individual occupies the top tier of importance.

induction: (adj., inductive) a process of reasoning that begins with particular data and draws a general conclusion or law.

idealism: the notion that reality is mental or somehow dependent upon mind for its existence and nature. Though idealisms emerged at many times, they share the common trait that reality is mental, rational, and all that is truly real lies beyond the material world.

Kant, Immanuel: (1724–1804) German philosopher of the Enlightenment and author of *Critique of Pure Reason* (1781) who created a watershed in modern philosophy. He integrated rationalism and empiricism into a unified epistemology that has inspired numerous philosophical movements.

Kierkegaard, Søren: (1813–1855) Danish philosopher, theologian, and pioneer of Christian existential thought.

libertarian free will: the idea that humans have the causal agency to do acts that are not wholly caused by natural laws acting upon them externally or internally. People are not controlled by divine determination. Thus people had the ability to do otherwise in choices they have made in the past.

Lucretius: (?-55 BCE) Roman poet and philosopher who wrote *De Rerum Natura* (*On the Nature of Things*) around 60 BCE. This work embraces the atomistic philosophy of the Greek philosophers Leucippus, Democritus, and Epicurus.

materialism: the idea that all reality is material. If anything exists at all, it must be material.

metanarrative: a master discourse, system, or worldview that claims to make judgments of objective truth over all other systems.

metaphysics: the field of philosophy that enquires into everything beyond or outside the scope of the natural sciences. It focuses on knowledge of the nonphysical, reason, first cause, ideas, concepts, essence, and universals. Materialists deny that such things exist.

modernity: an era of development in Western culture and philosophy beginning about 1640 and continuing up to Nietzsche.

monism: a system of thought that reduces all of reality to one single principle, usually matter or mind. Both materialism and idealism, though opposite, are monistic.

multiverse: a hypothesized reality beyond our universe that contains nearly an infinite number of universes. In each universe, the laws of physics work differently.

naturalism: the system of thought that claims the natural world alone exists. Naturalism holds that matter, natural laws, and physical forces can fully explain all realities. It denies a supernatural reality.

nihilism: affirms the meaninglessness of existence, knowledge, and morality. Though various forms exist, nihilisms affirm that nothing can be either known or valued objectively.

nominalism: a system of thought teaching that no universals exist and words are conventions. Thus things denoted by words have no essence.

overman: see *Übermensch.*

perspectivism: the notion that all truth claims arise from a perspective that is limited in scope and cannot capture the whole truth. No criteria exist outside of a system's perspective that can determine which system is true.

physicalism: the idea that all reality is physical, or reducible to physical characteristics. Something without physical traits is not real.

Plato: (427–347 BCE) Greek philosopher, student of Socrates, and founder of Platonism. Plato wrote prolifically on many philosophical topics using dialogues. His thought forms one of the major traditions of Western philosophy.

Platonism: Plato's system of philosophy, often called the Theory of the Forms. The forms are concepts or ideas that exist nonmaterially and beyond the material world, and they give everything being and character. Plato founded the Academy, which lasted many centuries and served as a prototype for the university.

positivism: an epistemological outlook dedicated to scientific and empirical knowledge as the only form of true knowledge. Truth claims that cannot be empirically verified cannot be knowledge.

postmodernism: a late twentieth-century movement employing perspectivism to undermine and deny any claims of fixed or absolute meaning in texts. Further, the movement denied any modern system's claim to know truth unaffected by culture, language, and prejudices. Reality, truth, and morality become inescapable social constructions.

presupposition: a tenet or belief assumed as a precondition for other beliefs. Often presuppositions lie unnoticed and uncovered, though they guide many other beliefs and actions.

psychoanalysis: a therapeutic method for diagnosing mental disorders established and pioneered by Sigmund Freud. Psychoanalysis explores and analyzes the unconscious mind through free association, often analyzing dreams.

rationalism: a major epistemological view that contends that knowledge lies in the innate structures of the rational mind. All knowledge comes primarily or exclusively through reason, not the senses. Descartes, Spinoza, and Leibniz led continental rationalism.

relativism: the belief that something has no absolute standards or criteria. Ethical relativism entails that there are no absolutes in ethics.

ressentiment: in Nietzsche this entails a slave's bitter animosity that cannot be openly expressed toward the master's domination. The clever slaves invent moral accusations of evil to lay upon the masters, effectively placing a guilt trip upon the masters to manipulate them into submission.

Schopenhauer, Arthur: (1788–1860) German philosopher, known for extreme pessimism, who claimed to be the only true Kantian after Kant. Deeply influenced by him, Nietzsche draws some ideas on the will from him.

Socrates: (470?-399 BCE) the great Greek philosopher and teacher of Plato. Socrates is the main protagonist in Plato's massive dialogues, who sets forth the platonic worldview. Often Socrates is considered the most iconic and influential philosopher of Western civilization.

theism: the belief that God exists.

transcendent: beyond human experience or something that lies outside and above the material and temporal world.

transvaluation (of values): in Nietzsche, the shifting of the definition of value from metaphysics and epistemology to the individual's will. This allows people to value what is beneficial for their life.

Übermensch: a distinctly Nietzschean concept, this "superman" or "overman" triumphs by will to power. The *Übermensch* evolves beyond weak human morality to found a new race. Many interpretations exist about what this term means.

utilitarianism: a normative ethical system that contends that all human actions should bring the greatest benefit to the greatest number of people. Thus the consequences of our actions determine what means and manner we should pursue.

virtue ethics: a normative ethical system that places character creation in a primary role. Virtue is for its own sake and is its own reward; it is not for duty or for its utility.

will to power: a distinctly Nietzschean concept, power and control propels people to dominate themselves or others. The *Übermensh* will employ will to power to ascend above all rivals and obstacles to dominate all and establish his own values for his own ends.

worldview: a belief system or way of seeing the whole, usually with a cluster of assumptions that we hold about the fundamental structure of everything. It gives a basis on which we understand everything.

Zeitgeist: the spirit of the times, or the traits and characteristics of an era.

Notes

In an effort to help readers locate Nietzsche's tweets for further reading in context, I will add the text location in brackets after the usual note with page numbers. This enables you to easily access his tweets using most published editions. Most of Nietzsche's texts appear as public domain on the Internet. I have used easily available English translations and editions. Kaufmann and Hollingdale produced most of the English translations.

Introduction

1. I have not included a biography due to space. For a reliable and standard biography of Nietzsche, I encourage readers to consult R. J. Hollingdale, *Nietzsche: The Man and His Philosophy*, rev. ed. (New York: Cambridge University Press, 1999). For the same reasons, a chronology is not included, but many are easily located.

2. Steven E. Aschheim, *The Nietzsche Legacy in Germany 1890–1990* (Berkeley: University of California Press, 1992), 45.

3. Perhaps Nietzsche's most read works are *Beyond Good and Evil* and *Thus Spoke Zarathustra*.

4. James W. Sire, *The Universe Next Door,* 5th ed. (Downers Grove: InterVarsity, 2009). Much of my insight into worldviews is indebted to this work through long use.

5. For a thorough exploration and history of worldview analysis, readers need look no further than David K. Naugle, *Worldview: The History of a Concept* (Grand Rapids: Eerdmans, 2002). However, readers will find a more accessible survey in James W. Sire, *Naming the Elephant: Worldview as a Concept,* 2nd ed. (Downers Grove: InterVarsity, 2015).

6. Sire, *Naming the Elephant*, 141.

7. Plato, *Apology*, 38a.

8. Friedrich Nietzsche, *Will to Power*, trans. Walter Kaufmann and R. J. Hollingdale (New York: Vintage, 1967), 18 [25].

9. Nietzsche, *Will to Power*, 550 [1067].

Chapter 1: Welcome to the Machine

1. Nietzsche, *Will to Power*, 550 [1067].

2. Frederich Albert Lange, *History of Materialism* 2nd ed. (Boston: James R. Osgood and Company, 1877); Hollingdale, *Nietzsche*, 69.

3. Friedrich Nietzsche, *The Gay Science* (1882) in *The Portable Nietzsche*, ed. and trans. by Walter Kaufmann (New York: Penguin, 1982), 95 [125].

4. "Theology: Toward a Hidden God," *TIME*: http://content.time.com/time/magazine/article/0,9171,835309,00.html#ixzz2saZmvFjo (accessed 12–5–2015).

5. Hollingdale, *Nietzsche*, 72.

6. http://www.pewforum.org/2012/10/09/nones-on-the-rise/ (accessed 3/3/2015).

7. Erich Heller, *The Importance of Nietzsche: Ten Essays* (Chicago: University of Chicago Press, 1988), 3.

8. Ibid., 26.

9. Friedrich Nietzsche, *Thus Spoke Zarathustra*, trans. with preface by Walter Kaufmann (New York: Modern Library, 1995), 261 [IV.6 "Retired"].

10. Nietzsche, *Gay Science* (1887), trans. Kaufmann, 447 [343].

11. http://www.pewforum.org/files/2013/04/051805-global-christianity.pdf (accessed 3/13/2014). See also, http://www.pewforum.org/2011/12/19/global-christianity-exec/(accessed 3/13/2014).

12. http://redcresearch.ie/wp-content/uploads/2012/08/RED-C-press-release -Religion-and-Atheism-25–7–12.pdf (accessed 3/17/2014).

13. http://www.pewforum.org/2015/11/03/u-s-public-becoming-less-religious/ (accessed 11/23/2015).

14. Nietzsche, *Gay Science* (1887), trans. Kaufmann, 448 [343].

15. Titus Lucretius Carus, *The Nature of Things*, trans. Frank O. Copely, (New York: W. W. Norton and Company, 1977), III. 866–69.

16. Nietzsche, *Zarathustra*, 13 ["Zarathustra's Prologue"].

17. Friedrich Nietzsche, *Beyond Good and Evil*, trans. by R. J. Hollingdale, with introduction by Michael Tanner (New York: Penguin, 1973), 32.

18. Plato, *Republic*, Book 7.

19. Alfred North Whitehead, *Process and Reality: An Essay in Cosmology* (New York: Free Press, 1978), Part II, Ch. 1, Sec. 1.

Chapter 2: What Do You Really Know?

1. Immanuel Kant, *Prolegomena*, ed. Paul Carus (Chicago: Open Court, 1949), 7.

2. Friedrich Nietzsche, *On Truth and Lie in an Extra-Moral Sense* (1873) in *The Portable Nietzsche*, ed. and trans. by Walter Kaufmann (New York: Penguin, 1982), 46–7.

3. Nietzsche, *On Truth and Lie*, 46.

4. Ibid., 47.

5. Nietzsche, *Gay Science* (1887), trans. Kaufmann, 449 [344].

6. Ibid., 449–50.

7. Friedrich Nietzsche, *On the Genealogy of Morals*, ed. Keith Ansell-Pearson, trans. Carol Diethe (New York: Cambridge University Press, 2006), 87 [III.12].

8. Paul Ricoeur, *Freud and Philosophy*, trans. D. Savage (New Haven: Yale University Press, 1970), 32.

9. Nietzsche, *Will To Power*, 267 [481].

10. Shakespeare, *Hamlet*, 1.3.564.

11. Friedrich Nietzsche, *Human All Too Human: A Book for Free Spirits* (1878), trans. Marion Faber in *The Nietzsche Reader*, ed. Keith Ansell Pearson and Duncan Large (Oxford: Blackwell, 2006), 162 [2].

12. Friedrich Nietzsche, *Twilight of the Idols: or How One Philosophizes with a Hammer* in *The Portable Nietzsche*, ed. and trans. Walter Kaufmann (New York: Penguin, 1982), 470 ["Maxims and Arrows" 26].

13. Nietzsche, *Zarathustra*, 152 [III.1 "The Wanderer"].

14. Nietzsche, *Beyond*, trans. Hollingdale, 65 [34].

15. Lucy Huskinson, *An Introduction to Nietzsche* (Peabody, MA: Hendrickson Publishers Marketing, 2009), 6–7.

16. Nietzsche, *Beyond*, trans. Hollingdale, 67 [36].

Chapter 3: Sailing Beyond Good and Evil

1. Nietzsche, *Twilight*, trans. Kaufmann, 467 ["Maxims" 8].

2. Ibid., 465 ["Preface"].

3. Friedrich Nietzsche, *Beyond Good and Evil*, ed. and trans. by Walter Kaufmann in *The Basic Writings of Nietzsche*, introduction by Peter Gay (New York: Modern Library, 2000), 405 [265].

4. I am indebted to Dr. Matt Mullins, associate professor of English, College at Southeastern, for his deep conversations with me about this film and his insights into it.

5. Nietzsche, *Will To Power*, 9 [2].

6. Roy Scranton, "We're Doomed. Now What?" *New York Times*, December 21, 2015, accessed December 21, 2015, http://opinionator.blogs.nytimes.com/2015/12/21/were-doomed-now-what/?_r=0.

7. Nietzsche, *Will To Power*, 14 [12].

8. Friedrich Nietzsche, *The Antichrist* in *The Portable Nietzsche*, ed. and trans. by Walter Kaufmann (New York: Penguin Books, 1982), 577 [11].

9. Nietzsche, *Beyond*, trans. Hollingdale, 96 [108].

10. Nietzsche, *Genealogy*, trans. Diethe, 25–6 [I.13].

11. Nietzsche, *Zarathustra*, 116 [II.12 "On Self-Overcoming"].

12. Ibid., 24 ["Zarathustra's Prologue" 9].

13. Ibid., 193 [III.11 "On The Spirit of Gravity"].

14. Ibid., 172 [III.5 "On Virtue That Makes Small].

15. Nietzsche, *Twilight*, trans. Kaufmann, 479 ["Problem of Socrates" 11].

16. Martin Seligman, *Authentic Happiness* (New York: The Free Press, 2002), 45ff.

17. Sigmund Freud, *Civilization and Its Discontents* (New York: W. W. Norton & Company, 1989).

18. Friedrich Nietzsche, *The Gay Science*, trans. Walter Kaufmann (New York: Vintage Books, 1974), 175 [116].

19. *Sheeple*: a portmanteau word fusing the sound and meaning of *people* and *sheep*, a common herd animal. *Sheeple* is my own nonce word, not Nietzsche's.

20. Nietzsche, *Antichrist*, 573 [7].

21. Ibid., 574 [7].

22. Friedrich Nietzsche, *Twilight of the Idols* in *The Anti-Christ, Ecce Homo, Twilight of the Idols, and Other Writings* ed. Aaron Ridley and Judith Norman, trans. Judith Norman (New York: Cambridge University Press, 2005), 194 ["Skirmishes of an Untimely Man" 5].

23. Friedrich Nietzsche, *Ecce Homo: How to Become What You Are*, trans. Duncan Large (New York: Oxford University Press, 2007), 88 ["Why I Am Destiny" 1].

24. Ibid., 489 ["Morality As Anti-Nature" 4].

25. Nietzsche, *Beyond*, trans. Hollingdale, 54 [23].

26. Jean-Jacques Rousseau, *The Social Contract*, trans. Maurice Cranston (New York: Penguin Putnam, 1968), 49.

27. Nietzsche, *Beyond*, trans. Hollingdale, 102 [146].

28. Pericles Lewis, *Religious Experience and the Modernist Novel* (Cambridge, UK: Cambridge University Press, 2010), 134.

29. Nietzsche, *Zarathustra*, 212 [III.12.26 "On Old and New Tablets"].

30. Ibid., 288 [IV.13.5 "On the Higher Man"].

31. Ibid., 100 [II.7 "On the Tarantulas"].

32. Plato, *Republic*, Book VIII.

33. Nietzsche, *Zarathustra*, 37 [I.5 "On Enjoying and Suffering the Passions"].

34. Nietzsche, *Twilight*, 476. ["Reconnaissance Raids of an Untimely Man" 22].

35. Nietzsche, *Beyond*, trans. Hollingdale, 37 [6].

36. Heller, *The Importance of Nietzsche*, 10.

37. Friedrich Nietzsche, *Daybreak*, ed. Maudemarie Clark and Brian Leiter, trans. R. J. Hollingdale (New York: Cambridge University Press, 1997), 88 [139].

38. Nietzsche, *Genealogy* (1887), trans. Kaufmann, 400 [I.10].

39. Michael Tanner, *Nietzsche: A Very Short Introduction* (New York: Oxford University Press, 1994), 87.

40. 1 Pet. 3:16–17 (NIV).

41. "But I tell you, do not resist an evil person. If anyone slaps you on the right cheek, turn to them the other cheek also." Matt. 5:39 (NIV).

42. Tertullian, *Apol.*, 50, 13.

Chapter 4: What Are We?

1. Nietzsche, *Zarathustra*, 34–5 [I.4 "On Despisers of the Body"].

2. Ibid., 12 ["Zarathustra's Prologue"].

3. William L. Shirer, *The Rise and Fall of the Third Reich: A History of Nazi Germany* (New York: Simon & Schuster, 1960), 91.

4. David B. Dennis, "Culture War: How the Nazi Party Recast Nietzsche," *Humanities* 35, no. 1 (January/February 2014), accessed April 2, 2014, http://www.neh.gov/humanities/2014/januaryfebruary/feature/culture-war.

5. Nietzsche, *Zarathustra*, 14 ["Zarathustra's Prologue"].

6. Ibid., 15.

7. Ibid., 288 [IV.13 "On the Higher Man"].

8. Nietzsche, *Genealogy*, trans. Diethe, 115 [III.25].

9. Nietzsche, *Zarathustra*, 157 [III.2 "On the Vision and the Riddle"].

10. Ibid., 59 [I.15 "On the Thousand and One Goals"].

11. Plato, *Theatetus*, 152a.

12. Nietzsche, *Zarathustra*, 210 [III.12 "On Old and New Tablets"].

13. Ibid., 17 ["Zarathustra's Prologue"].

14. Ibid., 93 [II.4 "On Priests"].

15. Ibid., 101 [II.7 "On the Tarantulas"].

16. Ibid., 185 [III.9 "The Return Home"].

17. Ibid., 79 [I.22 "On the Gift-Giving Virtue"].

18. Ibid., 286–7 [IV.13 "On the Higher Man"].

19. Nietzsche, *Beyond*, trans. Hollingdale, 43 [12].

20. Sebastian Gardner, "Nietzsche, the Self, and the Disunity of Philosophical Reason" in *Nietzsche on Freedom and Autonomy*, ed. Ken Gemes and Simon May (Oxford: Oxford University Press, 2009), 2–3.

21. Nietzsche, *Zarathustra*, 34 [I.4 "On the Despisers of the Body"].

22. Ibid., 31 [I.3 "On the Afterworldly"].

23. Todd Burpo with Lynn Vincent, *Heaven is for Real: A Little Boy's Astounding Story of His Trip to Heaven and Back* (Nashville: Thomas Nelson, 2010).

24. Mary C. Neal, M.D., *To Heaven and Back: A Doctor's Extraordinary Account of Her Death, Heaven, Angels, and Life Again: A True Story* (WaterBrook, 2011). Eben Alexander, *Proof of Heaven: A Neurosurgeon's Journey into the Afterlife* (New York: Simon & Schuster, 2012).

25. John Burke, *Imagine Heaven: Near-Death Experiences, God's Promises, and the Exhilarating Future That Awaits You* (Grand Rapids: Baker, 2015).

26. Nietzsche, *Zarathustra*, 316 [IV.18 "The Ass Festival"].

27. Dietrich Bonhoeffer, *Ecumenical, Academic, and Pastoral Work: 1931–1932*, edited by Eberhard Amelung, Christoph Strohm, Victoria J. Barnett, Mark S. Brocker, and Michael B. Lukens, trans. by Anne Schmidt-Lange, Isabel Best, Nicolas Humphrey, Marion Pauck, and Douglas W. Stott. Vol. 11. Dietrich Bonhoeffer Works (Minneapolis: Fortress, 2012), 219.

28. Ibid., 220.

29. Nietzsche, *Zarathustra*, 113 [II.12 "The Tomb Song"].

Chapter 5: Will to Power and Free Will

1. Heller, *The Importance of Nietzsche*, 8.

2. Nietzsche, *Beyond*, trans. Hollingdale, 194 [259].

3. William Barrett, *Irrational Man: A Study in Existential Philosophy* (New York, Anchor, 1962), 199.

4. Nietzsche, *Ecce Homo*, 35 ["Why I Am So Clever" 10].

5. Nietzsche, *Twilight*, 470 ["The Four Great Errors" 3].

6. Alan Alda, *Brains On Trial*, produced by Graham Chedd (PBS, 2013) accessed Mar 3, 2014, http://brainsontrial.com/.

7. Nietzsche, *Twilight*, 470 ["The Four Great Errors" 3].

8. Nietzsche, *Human*, trans. Hollingdale, 57 [106].

9. Ibid., [107].

10. Nietzsche, *Twilight*, trans. Kaufmann, 499 ["Four Great Errors" 7].

11. Sam Harris, *Free Will* (New York: Free Press, 2012).

12. Nietzsche, *Beyond*, trans. Hollingdale, 51 [21].

13. Nietzsche, *Twilight*, 542 [38].

14. Nietzsche, *Zarathustra*, 139 [II.20 "On Redemption"].

15. Ibid., 172 [III.6 "Upon the Mount of Olives"].

16. Nietzsche, *Human*, trans. Hollingdale, 57 [107].

17. Ibid. [106].

18. For a detailed survey of contemporary views on free will, see John Martin Fischer, Robert Kane, Derk Pereboom, and Manuel Vargas, *Four Views on Free Will* (Oxford: Blackwell, 2007).

19. Nietzsche, *Antichrist*, 572 [6].

20. Nietzsche, *Zarathustra*, 42 [I.8 "On the Tree on the Mountainside"].

21. Nietzsche, *Beyond*, trans. Hollingdale, 194 [259].

22. Ibid., 67 [36].

23. Nietzsche, *Zarathustra*, 112 [II.11 "The Tomb Song"].

24. Nietzsche, *Genealogy*, trans. Diethe, 120 [III.28].

25. Ibid., 68 [III.1].

Chapter 6: The Hourglass of Eternal Recurrence

1. Nietzsche *Ecce Homo: How to Become What You Are*, trans. with an introduction and notes by Duncan Large (Oxford: Oxford University Press, 2007), 65 [III "Z" 1].

2. Oswald Spengler, *Decline of the West* (New York: Alfred Knopf, 1926), xiv.

3. Nietzsche, *Zarathustra*, 158 [III.2 "On the Vision and the Riddle"].

4. Ibid., 166 [III.4 "Before Sunrise"].

5. Ibid., 221 [III.14 "The Convalescent"].

6. Ibid.

7. Mathias Risse, "The Eternal Recurrence" in *Nietzsche on Freedom and Autonomy*, ed. Ken Gemes and Simon May (Oxford: Oxford University Press, 2009), 224.

8. Nietzsche, *Zarathustra*, 221 [III.14 "The Convalescent"].

9. Nietzsche, *Gay Science*, trans. Kaufmann, 273 [341].

10. Giles Fraser, *Redeeming Nietzsche: On the Piety of Unbelief* (London: Routledge, 2002), 38–44.
11. Nietzsche, *Zarathustra*, 322 [IV.19 "The Drunken Song"].

Chapter 7: Let Freedom Ring

1. Nietzsche, *Zarathustra*, 286 [IV.13 "On the Higher Man"].
2. *The Third Man*, directed by Carol Reed (London: London Film Production, 1949), DVD (Lionsgate, 2010).
3. Friedrich Nietzsche, *Beyond Good and Evil*, ed. Rolf-Peter Horstmann, trans. Judith Norman (New York: Cambridge University Press, 2002), 90 [202].
4. Nietzsche, *Zarathustra*, 286 [IV.13 "On the Higher Man"].
5. Galatians 3:28.
6. Nietzsche, *Beyond Good and Evil*, 99 [126].
7. Nietzsche, *Beyond*, 194 [259].
8. http://www.unesco.org/culture/languages-atlas/index.php
9. Friedrich Nietzsche, *Untimely Meditations: On the Uses and Disadvantages of History for Life*, trans. R. J. Hollingdale, intro. J. P. Stern (Cambridge: Cambridge University Press, 1983), 83 [II 5].
10. Ibid., 95 [II 6].
11. Ibid., 79 [II 5].
12. Ibid., 94 [II 6].
13. Ibid.
14. George Orwell, *1984* (New York: Signet Classic, 1950), 37.
15. Nietzsche, *Untimely Meditations*, 95 [II 6].
16. Nietzsche, *Zarathustra*, 47 [I 10 "On War and Warriors"].
17. Ibid., 47.
18. Walter Kaufmann, *Nietzsche: Philosopher, Psychologist, Antichrist*, 4th Ed. (Princeton: Princeton University Press, 1974), 386–90.
19. Aschheim, *The Nietzsche Legacy*, 128–63.
20. Ibid., 143.
21. For a discussion on the appropriation of Nietzsche's ideas in World War I, see Watson, *Age of Atheism*, pp. 187–89.
22. Nietzsche, *Zarathustra*, 47 [I 10 "On War and Warriors"].
23. Ibid., 48 [I 11 "On the New Idol"].
24. Ibid., 49.
25. Mark Warren, *Nietzsche and Political Thought* (Cambridge: MIT Press, 1988), 213.
26. Ibid.

27. Nietzsche, *Zarathustra*, 50 [I 11 "On the New Idol"].
28. Ibid., 51.
29. Ibid.
30. Nietzsche, *Twilight* (1888), trans. Norman, 213 ["Skirmishes" 38].
31. Ibid.
32. Ibid., 221 ["Skirmishes" 48].
33. Nietzsche, *Zarathustra*, 212 [III.12 "On Old and New Tablets"].

Chapter 8: Nietzschean Insights on Life

1. Nietzsche, *Gay Science* (1882), trans. Kaufmann, 97 [283].
2. John F. Kennedy, "Moon Speech" (Sept. 12, 1962), http://er.jsc.nasa.gov/she/ricetalk.htm.
3. Homer, *Iliad*, Book 9:410.
4. Neil Young, "My My, Hey Hey (Out of the Blue)," *Rust Never Sleeps* (Reprise, 1979).
5. Nietzsche, *Beyond*, trans. Hollingdale, 58 [26].
6. Nietzsche, *Zarathustra*, 41 [I.7 "On Reading and Writing"].
7. Ibid., 55 [I.13 "On Chastity"].
8. Nietzsche, *Beyond*, trans. Hollingdale, 102 [146].
9. *Criminal Minds*, "Episode 200," episode 200, directed by Larry Teng, written by Jeff Davis and Rick Dunkle, CBS, Feb. 5, 2014.
10. Nietzsche, *Antichrist*, 612 [39].
11. Friedrich Nietzsche, *Human, All Too Human: A Book for Free Spirits*, trans. R. J. Hollingdale, intro. Richard Schacht (New York: Cambridge University Press, 1996), 28 [32].
12. Friedrich Nietzsche, *Human All Too Human: A Book for Free Spirits, Part II* trans. Paul V. Cohn, B.A. (New York: The MacMillan Company, 1913), 20.
13. Nietzsche, *Genealogy*, trans. Diethe, 119 [III.27].
14. Nietzsche, *Twilight*, 465 [Preface].
15. Nietzsche, *Ecce Homo*, 80.
16. Nietzsche, *Zarathustra*, 13 ["Zarathustra's Prologue"].
17. Rachel Carson, *Silent Spring* (Boston: Houghton Mifflin Company, 1962).
18. Nietzsche, *Gay Science,* trans. Walter Kaufmann, 98 [290].
19. Nietzsche, *Beyond,* trans. Hollingdale, 106 [175].
20. Nietzsche, *Twilight*, 475 ["Reconnaissance Raids of an Untimely Man" 19].
21. Ibid., 20.
22. Nietzsche, *Zarathustra*, 195 [III.11 "On the Spirit of Gravity"].
23. Ibid., 210 [III.12 "On Old and New Tablets"].

24. Ibid., 209.
25. Ibid., 40 [I.7 "On Reading and Writing"].
26. Neil Postman, *Amusing Ourselves to Death: Public Discourse in the Age of Show Business* (New York: Penguin, 1985).
27. Nietzsche, *Zarathustra*, 56 [I.14 "On the Friend"].
28. Nietzsche, *Ecce Homo*, trans. Anthony M. Ludovici in *The Complete Works of Friedrich Nietzsche* Vol. 17, ed. Oscar Levy (New York: Macmillan, 1911), 131 [IV 2].
29. Nietzsche, *Zarathustra*, 40 [I.7 "On Reading and Writing"].
30. Nietzsche, *Beyond*, trans. Hollingdale, 103 [156].

Chapter 9: A Deeper Dive into Nietzsche's Protean Worldview

1. Naugle, *Worldview*, 101.
2. Friedrich Nietzsche, *The Dawn* in *The Portable Nietzsche*, ed. and trans. Walter Kaufmann (New York: Penguin, 1982), 81 [101].
3. Nietzsche, *On Truth and Lie*, 46–7.
4. Nietzsche, *Will To Power*, 267 [481].
5. Nietzsche, *Twilight* (1888), trans. Norman, 203 [22].
6. Some of my insights owe credit to Ronald H. Nash, *Faith & Reason: Searching for a Rational Faith* (Grand Rapids: Zondervan, 1988).
7. *Apriori* means "before experience." *Aposteriori* means "after experience."
8. Heller, *The Importance of Nietzsche*, 13.

Chapter 10 Nietzsche and Naturalism

1. Nietzsche, *Twilight* (1888), trans. Norman, 178 ["The Four Great Errors" 3].
2. Nietzsche, *The Dawn*, 81 [123].
3. https://www.nasa.gov/content/finding-life-beyond-earth-is-within-reach (accessed 12/10/2015).
4. Antony Flew, *There is a God: How the World's Most Notorious Atheist Changed His Mind* (New York: HarperOne, 2007), 76–77.
5. Ibid., 78.
6. Multiverse theory evolves quickly with the fast pace of knowledge in quantum physics. Readers will find accessible explanations of these theories in Brian Greene, *The Hidden Reality: Parallel Universes and the Deep Laws of the Cosmos* (New York: Vintage Books, 2011) and Michio Kaku, *Parallel Worlds: A Journey Through Creation, Higher Dimensions, and the Future of the Cosmos* (New York: Anchor, 2005).
7. Nietzsche, *Ecce Homo*, trans. Large, 95 [IV 9].

Acknowledgments

M any encouraged me to write, and I remain indebted to them for their kindness. Some I have never met, but they have inspired me intellectually. Among those who directly encouraged me, I thank Bruce Ashford and Jamie Dew. Many colleagues—including Chip Hardy, Benjamin Quinn, and Steve Ladd—supported my efforts and insight. Mentors of many years also provided wisdom; among them I will always carry Dr. Thomas Porter's rhetorical insight and scholarly guidance. I also thank countless students who encouraged me to write. They daily instill hope for the future. My family, as is so often the case with authors, contributed heavily not only in encouragement, but in time. My wife, greatest of all, may heaven reward.

I heartily thank the College at Southeastern and Southeastern Baptist Theological Seminary for the gracious allowance of time to write.

I thank all who worked with me directly. My colleague Matt Mullins helped tremendously with conversations, editorial suggestions, and encouragement. Norman Miller's wordsmithing abilities guided me to sharpen the text and call me to a higher level of discourse. Darren Smith and Shawn Madden, both valued readers, anticipated and helped me avoid many pitfalls. Vivian Spencer, my daughter, provided many helpful rhetorical insights to reach my audience. Chief among those who labored diligently, I thank Billie Goodenough for proofing and suggestions. Each guided me away from errors and provided ideas that greatly enriched this work. For any oversights or shortcomings, I alone bear responsibility.